IT'S TIME TO BELIEVE

BELIEVE

By Gina Cannone

Cover by Leah Frieday

ISBN-13: **978-0692734988 (IbbiLane Press)**

ISBN-10: **0692734988**

This book is dedicated to my Mother who was also my best friend, Dolores.
You are missed with a longing too deep to express. Your belief in me and this project has kept me motivated even through my grief to complete this book on amazing true events that you have witnessed.
I feel you watching and guiding me. My love for you shall live forever.

Also, to my sisters Denise and Christina and my brother Peter whom I love more than life itself.

The purpose of this book is to help others believe, learn to pray and live a better life by listening to the Angels and Spirit Guides.

TABLE OF CONTENTS

FOREWORD

When I met Gina I was unhappy with my friends and how my life was going. Our conversations always went toward the spiritual side and how to make your life change. Gina was my mentor, I was struggling and the spiritual connection with her was amazing. I believed in Gina and looked up to her.

One day I was in the hospital from almost a nervous breakdown and drinking too much. I was at the lowest time of my life and wanted to give up and had suicidal thoughts. I started praying and thinking of what Gina told me, suddenly I had no fear and asked for what I wanted and needed. I felt a weird peaceful feeling and then prayed day and night for three weeks straight.

Suddenly, certain people appeared in my life and I was being surrounded by the people I needed. I heard a voice say, "You know" while I was awake. Gina always told me about Angels that guide and speak to her and when I heard the voice I knew it was a sign and was an instant knowing ability to what direction I should take my life.

Looking back, Gina was the most influential in getting me to change my life. She helped me plant the seeds and open the door so that I could see the signs. I believe that Gina was sent to me and her strong influence and spiritual connection got through to me.

Lisa LaPorta

When Gina was a small child, she always told me her dreams. At some point during the course of life, those dreams would happen. She would see apparitions and talk to the spirits on the other side.

Even witnessing this first hand, I still had my doubts. But, her prayers were always answered, her premonitions always happened and her messages from the other side for others were always true and amazing.

I have no choice, but to believe, she is my daughter and I have been shocked and amazed by her. She prays, she tells me her prayers and then it happens. Angels walk beside her, guide her and she always listens to them.

Dolores Talley (Mom)

AUTHOR'S PREFACE

Being Spiritual, a medium, psychic and clairvoyant has led me to writing this book. Friends and family have always said I should write down all these amazing stories, but as life gets busy it's put on the back burner. As I lay in bed one night I hear a faint voice say, "write the book. You have to write the book." It was a clear voice and I answered back, "Ok, I will."

This is a book about my answered prayers. It is also a book about how others can find fortune, happiness and loving relationships as I have, by learning how to pray sincerely and unselfishly, listening to your angels, and earning and expanding your good fortune through hard work.

The chapters in this book juxtapose amazing true stories from my own life with advice and guidance on how to make your prayers and wishes come true.

My stories start in my childhood, when I began to realize I was different. I could "see things" no one else could see, communicate with the unseen; even peer into the future. I felt the presence of guardian angels. The true events I relate range from funny to shocking to deeply scary. Incidents that will leave the reader saying, "This is unbelievable. This could not have happened." But it did.

The heart of this book is prayer ~intertwined with psychic and clairvoyant events. But also, this is a book for skeptics and those who are not yet in touch with their spiritual selves. You may not believe in angels, but they believe in you.

Gina Cannone

INTRODUCTION

First and foremost, I must say that I totally believe in the power of prayer. I believe we have Angels and Spirit Guides that are always with us. I believe that we can Pre-Pave our lives and set forth the motions and ground work needed to obtain our goals.

I have encountered and witnessed too many unexplained occurrences throughout my life not to question things and it is miraculous and enlightening. From an early age I knew I was what we call today 'intuitive' and remember saying I was 'open' to the spirit world. Many strange and unexplained events happened over the years. It took time to adjust to the visions, outer body experiences and the spiritual world.

I pray. I pray every night before sleeping. I pray for others and I listen very hard and eagerly to hear my messages.

In this book I will share with you the prayers I have said and the results of these prayers, along with other stories. What is most intriguing and miraculous about the praying and receiving, has been the amount of time it took to be answered. Each story is different and the same as you will read and I do believe all have the ability to pray and receive, if the strength and belief is within.

Along with the power of prayer there have been experiences that have happened that you may or may not believe. Nevertheless, they happened and you can take what you like from it, discuss and wonder. In this book are only true and actual occurrences that have happened in my life thus far…I have only to believe in a higher power, a God, an Entity, whatever you wish, because of these events. Even when my spirit is down, I can count on praying and receiving.

I have always wanted to share with others what I have experienced. I woke up the other day, anxious and stressed about everyday life decisions. Thoughts in my head kept repeating…but, I have received everything I've prayed for, why worry? So, I said a prayer and instantly felt calmer. I felt calmer because I know my prayers are always answered. I was also compelled to start this book and begin a new chapter in my life.

I hope you enjoy and take from this book a piece of the wonderment that you can use in life. A prayer, a true heartfelt prayer, can be heard and answered…

To have your prayers answered, Angels and Spirit Guides send messages, and receive all what you need and desire is amazing. I have endured many life difficulties and witnessed the outcome and effect of praying during those times. Prayer seems to be most needed and used when someone feels troubled, lost, sad, at the end of a situation, and for health and financial issues. These are perfectly great reasons to ask for help. But, I believe you can pray whenever needed. Even when life is good, pray to maintain that goodness. There is no limit of what you can ask for.

Our Angels and Guides are here for us all day and night. They want us to ask for help and guidance, that's what they are here to do. You can send what you ask for out into the universe, but, it is your Spirit guides and Angels that are listening and working hard for you.

The stories you will read are true and amazing. I am psychic medium and clairvoyant with a strong spiritual belief. These three components bridged together create an extremely high level of awareness and sensitivity to the unseen energy I can use. Clairvoyance means to see what may be coming. I pray for answers to those visions and receive message through a voice or dream. Having paranormal gifts has been just that: wonderful gifts. I respect the insight and visions of these gifts and always adhere and respond to them. My Angels and my Guides are honored and spoken to daily. They are the true messengers of my life that guide and carry me. Ask and you shall receive, seek and you will find. These stories all revolve around prayers, dreams and psychic events. The amazing results of answered prayers for myself and others, have been life changing.

I have prayed for myself and others, and what I prayed for wasn't easy. In every prayer was a real heartfelt energy sent out with the prayer. When I first received what I needed, I was amazed. I really needed and wanted what I asked for, but, deep down I didn't think it could happen. I got what I prayed for and it happened over and over again. I became more obsessed with talking to my Angels.

You can pray for answers to any questions and the answer will be sent to you. You must listen and when you hear it, acknowledge it. In some instances, you may not like the answers, but you should follow what you're told. The outcome is always for a forward moving direction of your life. I have seen apparitions, heard voices and personally have received everything I've prayed for. I have friends and family who have witnessed this throughout my life and who have realized that something out of the ordinary has happened.

Spirit Guides and Angels are here to assist us. Learn how to acknowledge and use them. Learn how to trust them and the decisions that are sent to you. I have never been let down. That is a big statement. The stories of what I asked for and received are amazing for many reasons. The difficulty of the situation and the results that I needed were demanding. I always believe that spirits of loved ones and Angels watch over us. I have seen them since I was young. I used to be very afraid, but time has removed the fear. I would love to see them more often, but they appear very rarely. I speak to them every day and count on them. I hear their voices; so different from your own inner voice talking. You will learn how to listen and hear it. They also count on me to follow the decisions sent and to help me work hard to achieve what I desire.

For instance, you can be sent a message to change jobs, but, if you don't look for that new job, you didn't acknowledge and act on it, so your life stays the same. I was sent a message to write this book. I didn't act on it right away, so the message came in again. My Angels and Guides already know I listen and hear, so by the second time I received the message, I acknowledged and acted on it. No matter what the messages are, it has been proven over and over again to trust and enjoy these messages, work for it and enjoy the outcome of every one of them. To learn how to pray, to speak to your Angels and Spirit guides, to ask for it and receive it, is powerful. There are no walls, no boundaries and no limits for asking. After learning how to speak to them and how to ask for what you want, you will get your answers and you will get sent to you all that you desire. Your belief in your ability to achieve, succeed and do the work, will allow all to come to you.

You will learn how to dig deep into your soul and inner being to find this out. You will learn how to get it, act on it and keep it, by constantly trusting the messages sent to you. We are sent so many messages and opportunities, but, most don't listen and throw them away. Some of you probably hear those voices from time to time, but fear, doubt, money and life get in the way. I believe in miracles, I believe in prayer, I believe everyone should get what they ask for, and respect it and treat it like a delicate gift, because it is a gift. These stories are extraordinary; people have witnessed the results with awe. Non-believers have listened, learned and now believe. The more you believe, the more you trust, the more you ask, the more you will get. The door is open to receive all the opportunities and desires the world has to offer.

Therefore I tell you,
Whatever you ask for in prayer,
Believe that you have received it-and it will be
yours.

Mark 11:24

CHAPTER 1

CONSCIOUSLY BEGIN

To consciously begin this process of pre-paving and
visualizing your life will take some serious thinking time.
Your inner guidance system is usually always on track, so
search first for your true wants and desires. Whatever age
you are, you can start this process immediately. Sometimes
it is a natural thought without any effort that will just keep
creeping into your mind. One example of this in my life has
been the constant thought of living on or by the beach all
year round. This thought process started and

I would say repeatedly that I was going to find a way to
accomplish this. I visualized beach condos and homes and
always bought Florida magazines. I then started to say I
want a condo on the beach. Well, this was a constant
visualization in my life. I prayed for this and the thought
remained. How was I to do this? I prayed for extra work to
come my way. It did and I worked harder than ever and
started to save for a down payment. I was now pre-paving
my destiny mentally and physically. I was obsessed with
getting this. The day came when I woke up one morning
and heard a voice say, go to Florida and start looking. I did
go to Florida and found the condo of my dreams on the
beach. I now had the panic set in. Should I do this? Will I
be able to afford it and keep it? Will I be able to use it often
enough? I stopped and took a breath and prayed. I asked for

guidance and assurance and asked for answers. When you believe in this process of pre-paving and praying, you will be amazed how you are guided and will hear the messages. I heard the answers and felt immediately calm. My head was flooded with answers. You *worked* for it, it's what you always *wanted* and *prayed* for, and you can afford it. So, I bought it.

When you decide what it is that you really want and picture yourself in that life it is the beginning of pre-paving your life. This is how you consciously begin. Start with one desire, and know that after practice you will be able to ask for it all. Once you decide to start and then actually see and hear what is sent to you for you to achieve it, it will then create more energy for the receiving of it. You must know exactly what you want before praying for it.

Here are the steps to Consciously Begin:

- Decide on the want and desire
- Visualize it
- Keep it a constant thought
- Be ready to work for it
- Pray for it, know why you want it and deserve it
- Learn to see and hear the messages and signs sent to you
- Know what to do when you get it

I was amazed at what I had accomplished. You may think, 'Oh, she just worked hard to get it - no big deal', but this was in my thought process constantly. Even when I was busy and had no time to think about it, it would pop up. A strong want and desire does just that. It keeps haunting you. Listen to it. It is there for a reason. This desire didn't stop at this point either.

I have been enjoying my beach condo and now every time I leave I say, "I should be living like this all the time." Now that thought process has started. It now remained strong and it became a *want*. I had a dream one night that I was living somewhere by the beach in a beautiful condo. The predominant feature of it was the floor to ceiling windows. I thought it was a vision that I was going to move to my Florida condo. I am clairvoyant and do see future events. I was not ready to move and the time period when these visions will occur are still unclear. I envisioned this a few times. This too remained a very strong thought and vision. Approximately fourteen months later I moved into this wonderful condo across the street from the ocean in New Jersey, with 10 ft. oversized floor to ceiling windows. It happens to be an end unit and the windows are the dominant feature and are magnificent.

I stood there the first day I moved in and cried. I was so happy and thought…"I always wanted to live full time by the ocean." This had been embedded in my thoughts from the beginning, that's why it didn't stop with the Florida condo. It had to finish. I believe I was guided and that I listened to myself and my Angels along the way.

Opening yourself to the spirit world and believing you can pray and receive what you ask for is the foundation of pre-paving one's way. The power of prayer and receiving messages is amazing. Sometimes I must think for days, maybe even weeks or months, on something I might want to pray for. Being aware and consciously putting in effect the desires starts the delivery. I pray for myself, family and friends. I must know exactly what they want if it's for them.

I have this paranormal gift and I do not confuse it with my messages from my angels. They are quite different from each other. I visually see a picture or a flash in my head during a clairvoyant vision. I know it will happen but I don't know when. When I hear messages or see signs sent to me it is like having a person standing next to me. The voice can be faint, but it's still heard. It takes time to hear it at first, but becomes clearer with time. It's hard to explain this. The signs are also very clear. I believe we are guided to get where we need to be and to stay on track in our lives. Our guides and Angels know what we need to be happy and balanced. We know what we need. We can have what we want and need but the normal thought process is to be negative and think it's too difficult. We are influenced wrongly by outsiders that also have negative undertones. Remove these negative people and thoughts and you will see change.

I prayed for my sister one night. She had very hard years in her life and wanted a simple home life. She only wanted a husband and one child. Simple, right? It wasn't happening for her. The want and desire was there. She only thought about this and the obsession process was in effect. She however, was not meeting the right men and was asking for help. She was extremely upset and we were worried about her.

I lay in bed one night and began my prayers. This night was to be a special night for praying. I prayed for my sister, and asked that she be sent what she needed. I also prayed that she gets what was coming my way also. I gave up what I wanted and asked that it be given to her. I prayed with tears in my eyes that she be taken care of and given a child. She was unable to make it alone, I knew I could and would as long as she received what she wanted. I wanted her happiness to be fulfilled. This prayer was one of the most meaningful, unselfish, most heartfelt prayers I have ever prayed.

The very next evening, I was out with my boyfriend and a friend of his stopped by the house. We were all talking and he asked if I had any nice single friends. I said yes, quite a few. I happen to have just picked up pictures of all of us from the weekend before and told him to take a look at all (8) of the girls and let me know which one he liked. He spent a minute and pointed to my sister in the photo and said that's the one I want. I said, look again, take your time and let me know again. He said, no, I want to go out with her only. Ok, I set up dinner for the next night. They met and talked the entire evening. They were inseparable from that day on, got married and she had one child, a girl, named Victoria.

Now, before Victoria was born, I prayed and thanked the Lord for answering my prayer and taking care of my sister. I also asked for a sign that this child would have a connection to me, for I knew I wasn't going to have children of my own. I wanted a piece of me with her, I can't really explain what this feeling was that I was asking for, but it did get explained eventually.

Victoria was a beautiful baby. She was the first grandchild to be born and brought such happiness to all of us. The years were good and happy for my sister and Victoria is now around the age of four. One day I was watching her while my sister was shopping and we were playing and laughing. She looked up at me and stared in my eyes and said, "Aunt Gigi, I remember when you broke your tooth, remember?" Our eyes were locked together. I said, "What?" She said, "Remember, I was there." I thought I was going to faint. I said, "Yes, I broke my tooth, which one was it?" She took her little finger and touched the front tooth that was broken when I was seven years old. As she was pointing and touching my tooth, she kept saying, "That one; remember, I was there."

I waited a few minutes in shock and then asked her again- which one was it? She sighed, like I was annoying her and said "I told you, that one". The entire time she kept her eyes locked on me, like I have never seen before from a child. I was nervous and excited that this happened. I called my sister and asked her if she had ever mentioned this to her. My sister said, "Why would I tell my four year old about your tooth? Why are you asking me this?" I told her what happened and she was completely floored. I received my answer from the prayer. It was sent to me through my niece with something that would be undeniably difficult to explain. I accept the confirmation from above and will always be there for her.

If you believe and want something, it is yours to get. Just knowing what will make you happy and feel balanced will begin the positive reactions in your life. I pray and expect to receive. I trust the timing of things. It will come when the time is right. I have prayed for things to come quickly and they have. Everything starts with a thought. Sometimes the thought comes from someone else. Was that a sign? People and ideas cross paths for reasons. The steps for achieving and obtaining it all, takes time and patience and usually work. Do you remember an idea or opportunity that came your way and you passed it up? Looking back, you might think you should have tried or started the process of getting it done. Many pass up what is sent and don't see it or even worse; see it and let it go. You need to learn to trust what is in front of you and why it is there. Pray and ask for answers, they will be answered. You must make it a part of your daily life and routine to be aware of all that is around you. It may seem like more things to think about and more to obsess about, but it is for the life you want and desire. I can't think of anything better to think about. The more you work on these thoughts of getting the life you want, the easier it gets. It will come naturally on a daily basis and become a part of your existence with no interference.

Enjoying the process and being amazed as the reality of it comes to fruition creates more positive energy. The good energy just keeps feeding itself to get you closer to happiness and fulfillment. But beware because the same goes for the opposite. It is important to control and reverse any negativity and outside influences that will confuse you and get you off track. Avoid all and even totally remove any person or thing that may hold you back from your goals, happiness and well-being. Surround yourself with good people, people who will help, guide and support you. Speak to your loved ones who have passed on and talk to your Angels. They are here to guide and protect.

This leads me to a story about removal of negativity. I got engaged, traveled to Europe, visited all the churches and galleries. I absorbed it all. This person I was with was money driven and stated that art was a waste of time.

He would say I would never be a good enough artist or make any money at it. I also was studying piano at that time and again, he said I would never play well and was wasting time on it. All I kept hearing was negative responses towards the actions I was taking for my happiness. What did he care what I was doing with *MY TIME* anyway? I certainly wasn't interrupting his time. No matter what I was doing to achieve what I wanted, he would disrupt, annoy, aggravate and try to discourage me from obtaining it.

Many people may be in this situation at any given point in their life. What do you do about it? *Can* you do something about it? Do you want to do something about it? I asked myself these questions. I first knew I *wanted to do something about it.* Then I decided I could do something about it. I decided to ask this man one more time, "Why do you keep discouraging me and not supporting me?" The response was the same negative tone. I walked out of the room in silence and shut the door behind me. Now, I was getting very upset just being around this person and started to withdraw from him. This happened over a six month period. I was very sad that I was with someone who was so negative. This was not what I wanted for my life. I was becoming an accomplished piano player and still focusing on my goals, but had to fix this situation. It was jealousy on his part setting in. My time was being spent on studying and I was getting good at it. One night, as I lay in bed, I heard a faint voice ask, "What are you doing?" It was quite clear and right next to me. I actually turned my head. Deep down I knew what I was being asked. I replied, "I'm thinking." I heard the message, "Go back home and leave." I heard this message a few times while trying to sleep.

So I say a prayer:

> Please, give me the courage to do what I have to.
>
> I will listen to the message.
>
> Just give me the strength to follow through and leave.
>
> No matter what, help me to do this, I know I have to leave and I want to leave.

It took about a week to get the courage up, but I did exactly what I was told by my angels. I packed up while he was working. I decided to tell him as soon as he got home. I remember this like it was yesterday. I was in the kitchen and he walked in. I was really nervous and a little scared. I felt a nudge. I took my foot and drew an imaginary line with it on the floor. I said to myself, once you cross the line, never turn back. I stood there for one second, walked over it and left to start my life again on track.

This was a strong action and move. I was young, but knew what I wanted for my life. Or at least, I knew what I didn't want. It was one of the first basic steps I needed to do and learn that would mold me forever. I would never again have a hard time removing negativity from my life. It may not be easy sometimes and it may be sad sometimes, but it's worth it. Trying to fix the issues is the first option and removal of it the final option. I never looked back and it was the beginning of my art and music career. My happiness began the day I was driving back home with only a few of my things and my cat, Annie.

So, now I am living in New York, working in a salon during the day and trying to make it as an artist at night. I was getting small art jobs from friends and clients and now working hard at both. I was asked to donate a few art pieces for the local hospital charity event and I did. That night, a designer asked me to work for her and I started that week. I was now getting busy with my art and murals and needed to make a big decision. How do I give up my full time salon clientele that pays my mortgage and bills, to work full time as an artist, not knowing whether I can make enough? I had money saved, but didn't want to ever touch it. I prayed a lot and needed an answer. That week my mother said, "Take this chance, if you get stuck along the way with money I will help you. You are too talented not to try as hard you can to make it if this is what you are supposed to do. You were born with talents and you have to use them."

So, I plunged in, working some weeks and some not, painting murals, faux finishing, detailing moldings and columns, etc. I was not making enough, and dipped into those savings I swore I would never touch. I was too proud to take from my mother, but I just felt comforted knowing if I was desperate I could. I worked hard at not ever having to ask her. So, I dipped into my savings even more. A year had passed by and I was getting very nervous about my decision. Give it six more months, I said in my head. At the fifth month I lay in bed crying to the Lord, "Please, I know I am good, why am I not getting more work?" I lay awake all night that night. I remember it as if were yesterday. I heard a voice say, "How can they see what you do by meeting you?"

I thought about it and realized I had no cards or flyers with pictures on them. I also had no money left. I went to a printer that week with photos of some work and asked for a flyer to be designed. He said the work is amazing but you'll need it in color for people to appreciate it. I asked for some prices and there were stipulations on color and quantity. The price was thirty-eight hundred dollars. I almost fainted. I said, "Give me a minute" and I walked outside to get calm. I looked up, and said, "GOD, please make this be ok." I asked my angels to guide me. I heard again, just do it. I only had about five thousand dollars in the bank and I walked back in and said ok. Of course, I had buyer's remorse and cried a few times that week. My mother couldn't believe I would go through all my savings and then use the last of it for this business. I said, "I know this is what I needed to do."

The flyers and business cards came in and they were beautiful. Everywhere I went, I put a few. At restaurants, in bathrooms, on countertops at stores; I had no shame where I put them. That month was the beginning of my career towards the artist I am today. I was flooded with work. I had numerous articles written on me. I won awards, donated work, and began to get recognition.

I never lost faith and when praying the answers were always there. You just need to be open, calm and listen. I like to spend 20 minutes of alone time and meditate and think about what it is I should pray for. I never pray for money. The first question people ask is, "Why don't you pray to win the lottery?" I laugh and tell them it really doesn't work like that. Not for me, anyway. I pray for work to come my way, I pray for opportunities to cross my path and know when to take them. I will always do what I need to do when set in front of me. I always promise in my prayers that I will do the hard work necessary if given the chance.

Have you ever been given an opportunity that you passed up because you did not want to do the work required to make it happen? I pray that if given these opportunities I will do the work and I know that it will become a reality or dream come true. I have no doubt.

I remember my mother asking me, "Who are you waiting for?" I showed her a list of what I wanted in a partner and she said, "That's a tall order!" and laughed. I explained that I had to really think about what I need and then I can pray for it. So, that night, I prayed for this person. I asked the Lord to send me what I needed and I will be patient.

You see, I don't know when the prayers are going to be answered, but surprisingly, it has always happened within a short time and mostly within days! Well, the next day, I was with a client and he said, "You need to meet my partner, he's perfect for you." I asked him a lot of questions and this person met all my criteria. So, he set it up and that night his partner Sal, had called me. We talked for an hour and made plans to meet the next evening in New York City where he lived. I had to cancel that night.

He had to cancel the next time. I couldn't make it the next time; this went on for seven dates. Finally, we met, had dinner and ended up together for the next thirteen years.

My list was demanding, not a normal request. I wanted a man who was a businessman, smart, funny, exciting, well-traveled, liked to played tennis, ski, own a boat, love the ocean and beach, love fine dining and cooking. Well, like I said, he met all the criteria and was sent to me the very next day.

I believe it is very important to think before you pray and know exactly what you are praying for. I have prayed with doubt in my head and those prayers are never answered. When I know exactly what I am praying for, the miracle happens.

It was time to get a bigger home and sell my townhouse. I had people in and out and got this buyer who just would not put any money down. He kept saying next week, next week. Well that night when praying, I asked God: "Why can't you just send me a cash buyer? That's what I need right now. Please, make this easy for me." The next day, an elderly Italian couple knocked on my door. They said, "We would like to buy your house." I replied, "But you haven't seen it." They said, "Can we see it now? We have been in others and want to buy here." So, I let them in, they loved it, and they wanted it. I was shocked and in disbelief. I said, "Ok, we have to go to the realtors office and do paperwork and you have to put money down." They agreed, followed me over there, wrote a check, and said they were paying cash! Unbelievable! My strength for praying was getting stronger and even I couldn't believe it all. To this day I hear from them time to time and they tell me how much they love living there.

That brings us to the next house. My good friend Tom owned a beautiful center hall colonial. When we were all single and having fun, he would throw many parties in his house. One night I told him, "I'm going to live here one day." Every time I saw him or was at his house, I would say, "This is going to be my house." I started the pre-paving process for this house. It was on my mind and I was definitely going to live there one day. When I was at his house, I would look around and figure out how I was going to decorate it. He would laugh at me and say, "You're crazy! I'm not leaving until I find a girl to marry and have a baby." So, of course, every girl he goes out with, I say, "She's great, marry her." He would crack up laughing and reply, "I'll let you know." Anyway, many girls later, he finally finds the one he wants to marry. They have the wedding, she gets pregnant, and he still doesn't leave. He decides to stay and I forget about his house now and pray that I figure out where to move to.

I prayed that evening. "Lord, Please, please, help me figure this out, I *really wanted* Tom's house, help me decide where to go now." I practically had tears in my eyes. Believe it or not, there was no other house I wanted. It was two blocks from my parents, the size and space was perfect and I had been praying for it for a long time. I had fallen asleep disturbed about not having that house and asking for some answers.

The next night, Tom calls me. "Gina, we decided to move to NJ, do you still want my house?" I couldn't believe my ears. "Are you kidding with me?" He said, "No, we want to move." We all went out that night, shook hands, and Sal and I lived there for thirteen years. Sal has since passed away suddenly, and has been with me and guiding me. I have seen his apparition only once and it was for a split second. My prayers and spirituality were in full force and my visions were increasing also.

Attracting what you need and want starts with thinking about it. I've said this before but truly thinking about what, where and how you want your life to be is crucial to receiving it. Consciously begin to routinely think about your list. Everyday take time to evaluate and meditate on it. Every night, pray for these desires and sincerely want them for all the right reasons.

When I have prayed and missed some details, the prayer was answered with those details missing. I have only recently started to pray in great depth and detail. I have received all of it thus far. A wonderful prayer story to illustrate this is when I prayed for my boyfriend. I was now dating again, and was alone for over a year after Sal passed. I prayed for what I needed, but left some details out. I was sent people who fit half of my criteria of what I wanted. As each very nice man came along, I realized what I wasn't praying for. Finally, I figured it out. I now speak my elaborate prayer. I held my palms face up, and started with exactly what I wanted. I also asked that it come quickly. I asked for this special someone to be:

- 6ft or taller
- Have no hair
- Great lips
- Not skinny –not fat-football type
- Be funny
- Be super nice
- Be generous and giving in all ways
- Have a great family that I would love
- If he had kids I wanted girls only between ages 9-11
- Have a good job
- Likes to travel; short trips only
- Can handle my poker playing
- Lives close by
- Then I added that it's not a deal breaker but if he plays tennis that would great

Well, two days later my best friend calls me and says, "I have this person that is going to call you. He's perfect for you and he wants to take you out tonight." I thought she was crazy. I was in no mood to go out that night, but he called and didn't give me a chance to say no. I figured, oh well, it's a Monday, I'll go out to dinner. I meet him, we go to dinner and by the end of the night I knew he was sent.

I am always in awe when a prayer is answered. It is witnessing miracles all the time. After receiving this, I then hear those shallow voices, saying, "You have to give time and energy to what you asked for. We sent him, now give him the energy required for a relationship to grow or you will be tossing it away." This meant something to me. I do have a hard time giving my full energy and time to another person, especially a new relationship. I am the type to be selfish with my own time because I always have projects on the table that I need to do. Those projects usually require a lot of my time and when I am focused I tend to put relationships second. I listened to that message. This time, I gave my energy equally and sometimes more to him and his family and now have a beautiful person to share my life with.

Here's what to do:

- Consciously begin to create your life as you want it to be. Start your day with positive thoughts and attitude. Decide that the day will be great no matter what.
- Consciously begin to look at the people in your life. Can and will they help you achieve? Are they supportive and positive? Do they hinder and or hold you back? You will have to decide to 'clean house' as I call it and focus on developing new relationships that will help you grow.
- Consciously begin to have faith or renew your faith. Speak to your Angels and ask for guidance. Do this

until it becomes routine. Start by spending ten to fifteen minutes on thinking about your life and where you want it to go.

- The more you think and meditate on the positive and what you want to achieve, the more you will receive. Ask to be sent the right people to help you. Ask for it to go smoothly and with ease. Promise to work hard and to use it all wisely.
- Become obsessed and focused on creating your life. Ask for energy to complete the tasks.
- Consciously start to think of the beginning and the end. When you think about everything with total completeness, you will see it come into your life.

Change the direction of your life. Start your list with enthusiasm and without any doubts. Take each task as is comes and listen to yourself. You and only you know what exactly what it is you want and how you want your life to change.

I have set forth motion of the pre-paving process for approximately 85 % of everything I have achieved. The other 15 % of it was started by an outsider. I was sent opportunities that I knew I had to take. The messages were so clear and the flow and ease of the start of it meant there was a reason for me to see it and take it. The more thought I put into visualizing and obtaining my goals, the quicker it came to me. I know speaking to my Angels and constantly asking them to protect and guide all that I do keeps things going smoothly and on track.

It is much harder to be positive in this world than to be negative. The first challenge to remember is to be positive and clear on your thoughts. There will always be negative attitudes and disruptions that will want to set you back. I have learned to just not allow any of it into my life. I'm not saying I don't get annoyed or upset about anything, of course I do, but it is definitely a short lived moment. I immediately say a prayer. I instantly decide to change the direction of the negative feeling to a positive starting point. I ask myself, how can I change this and how quickly can I do it? Yes, it is very difficult sometimes, and when I can't change it quick enough, it does get worse. Once you learn how to manipulate your own thoughts to focus only on positive intentions you will then begin the process of planning life's new path with exceptional energy and will power.

Consciously begin to acknowledge when a negative response or feeling enters your thoughts. Ask your guides, "Why am I feeling like this?" There's usually a reason. Is the reason good enough to warrant these negative thoughts? Are you just impatient? Are you holding a grudge? Are you giving in to fears? I go through this process of questioning periodically myself.

This is when I take a deep breath and pray. I pray that I stay calm and patient. I ask that I remain focused and positive. I pray that my goals and needs come as quickly as they can, and that I will wait patiently for all the pieces to fit properly. I know it takes time and effort for everything to be complete. Usually, we start something and then negative interference and doubt set in. This is where belief and strength is now needed most. I depend and count on it with my entire being without any doubts. It has never failed me and it works. The more I think and speak about my goals and the more I pray is when they manifest in my life. It is amazing to be so aware and watch it all just flow into your reality. As each piece is set in front of you your belief gets stronger. You will want to pray more and talk to your Angels and guides more. The more you do all of this, the closer you come to obtaining it. The path that you have thought about and visualized is now taking effect. It is an exciting process to realize that it can change and set your life in the direction toward your goals.

Will there be set backs? You may think a setback is a negative. Back to the first challenge you must go! Change that thought to understand that the setback is part of the process. Let's figure out what and why the setback occurred. Will a new thought or input make completion stronger than what would originally have taken place? Or perhaps a little more time was needed to make it right. So, now do you still think the setback is a negative? By believing the course of motion has a pace needed for completion, you will learn patience. That, too, is as difficult as staying positive.

I am presently waiting for completion of one of my goals. Am I and everyone else involved in this project anxious? Yes we are. But, it's funny how we all are helping each other stay calm. We take turns helping each other stay positive and focused. The only thing to do right now is to keep positive thoughts in motion and wait patiently. I did say a prayer for myself. I needed to relax and acknowledge that this waiting period is important. My message came in after my prayer. I was told to enjoy this time for I will miss it one day. I thought, wow, miss it? Yet I knew what it meant: I'd be missing it in a good way. That faint voice that is heard is ever so quiet, but loud at the same time. My inner voice doesn't talk like that. That's how you will start to know the difference between your own inner voice and a message from your Guides and Angels. I believe people hear and see what they need to but disregard it for many reasons, mostly for all negative reasons.

If you want something badly enough, obsess about it, visualize it, crave it, talk about it, work for it, ask and pray for it. Believe in yourself, believe in your Angels and believe you deserve it.

CHAPTER 2

UNCONSCIOUS LISTENING

I woke up one morning after a night of having a horrendous nightmare. The dream was that I was driving on the Garden State Parkway in my truck, traveling around 60 miles per hour in the left lane and as I tried my brakes they weren't working. I looked to my right and saw a family in an SUV with children looking back at me. I then looked to my left and saw there was a pole. I heard a voice in my dream say, "If you hit the vehicle next to you, you will live, but someone in the other vehicle will die". So, I looked at those children again, turned the steering wheel to the left, hit the pole and woke up. When I woke up, remembering this dream, I thought it was a test from the other side to see what I would do in regard to the value of another life. I thought, 'great, I passed'.

The next night while sleeping, this dream reoccurred, and once again, I chose the same path to hit the pole and die. That morning though, I just really wondered why I had this dream again but the day got started and I went to work and forgot about it.

For the third night in a row, this dream occurred again. This time the children's faces are quite clear and frightened. I turned the steering wheel again to the left and hit the pole head on at full speed, died and in an instant my spirit left my body and watched over the horror. I woke up right away and sat straight up in my bed. It was early, but I got up anyway, made coffee and started to try and think about this. I thought, why three nights in a row? Why did I have to feel the impact as if were real and die? Why did my spirit leave my body and hover over the scene? I knew this was going to be on my mind all day.

I had to get to work and finish an art job. It was a Wednesday and I got in my truck and sat for a minute. I spoke out loud and said, I know my brakes are working fine, they are not making any strange noise, what is this dream about? I heard a voice answer, do not drive on highways. These voices are soft spoken whispers and can be very hard to hear if you're not listening but I heard it. Do not drive on highways. Now, I have to work Wednesday and Thursday and I would normally use the highways. Friday I was off. I'm sitting in my truck wondering what to do. I decided to put a sticky note on my steering wheel, saying, 'Do not drive on highways'. I spent the next two days avoiding the parkway and highways and travelled the side streets. Yes, it was an inconvenience but I always listen to these messages that are sent even if I don't understand them at the time.

I made it. It's Friday morning. I didn't have the reoccurring dream of my tragic automobile death. My brakes were working perfectly and I am off for the day. I get in my truck and look at the note that is still there. I heard that faint voice speak: go get the truck checked. I am a seasoned listener of these voices. It takes time to hear them and more time to actually listen to them and do what they say. I really didn't want to do this on my day off and anyone else who would not usually listen to such a voice but would go on with their normal day. But I have to listen. So I drive to my friend who owns a Midas dealership up the road. I ask him to check my brakes. He asked me, "Why? Are they making any noises or feel like they are not working right?" I said, "No, everything feels fine, but I need you to check them anyway." He seemed hesitant, so I asked again, "Please just look at them for me, I'll pay for the time it takes to check them."

I am in the waiting area while he puts the truck up on the lift. After about ten minutes he comes into the waiting area where I was sitting. He looked at me and said, "I don't know how you knew to come here, there are no sounds or outward problems with your brakes, but ALL four of your brake pads are out. You would have been driving and just would have had no brakes. There were no signs just pressing on the brakes that could have warned you so what made you come here?" I told him, "I dreamt three nights in a row that I died while driving and it was because of brake failure, and my Angels told me to check them." He was amazed and said this would be one of those stories he was going to tell for the rest of his life.

Dreams that you remember, I feel, all have important messages that are sometimes hidden or if you're lucky very clear. Those that are in tune with their dreams will seek out to find the messages. My dream about the car brakes was a warning dream. Angels and Spirit Guides watch over us and help us with things that we may have no control or knowledge about. Everyone dreams, some remember their dreams, some don't. If you remember them, write them down as soon as you wake up and acknowledge them. Messages through dreams are powerful and wonderful. You can ask to be sent messages while sleeping, and trust they will come. You can dream and envision how you want life to be, starting the pre-paving process toward a new life.

Whether awake or sleeping, your inner guidance system is always in effect. You may hear that faint voice or you can feel something within your system that guides you to your thinking process. The messages can come to you while awake or sleeping. Everyone has the capability of receiving these messages and if you want life to be as you want it, you need to listen and evaluate these messages so that you can make solid decisions for your life.

As you learn to hear your Angels and Guides, they will come in louder and clearer. It will be as if someone is right by you holding your hand and telling you what to do. Within time, you will count on your Guides and Angels, and they will be even more helpful. Things will flow and come to you easily. Your life will be directed, but it will be up to you to act and do your part. If you follow what is put in front of you, life will change. If you discard the messages, at best your life will remain the same. If you pray for desires, if you pray for help and guidance, then you obviously believe they could be answered, otherwise *why pray?* If you believe that prayers can be answered and you can be sent what you need, now you have to hear and listen to what they are saying.

I receive messages constantly. I receive them awake and I receive them while sleeping through dreams. I am at a level of complete trust with my guidance system and my Angels. I consistently pray for what I want and deserve and I am thankful for all that I already have and will have. Being thankful for something you haven't received yet may boggle you. When I pray, I say that I will appreciate it when it comes my way, I will know when I have it in front of me, and I will cherish it and do what I am supposed to when I receive it. This is important, because it is human nature to wish or pray for something, but when it starts to come your way, you toss it aside. I have witnessed friends doing this many times, and wonderful opportunities have passed them by.

I ask for guidance every day and to be sent what I need. If there is a problem that I am not sure how to fix, I ask my Angels to send me answers. I ask for guidance in making the right decision. I ask that when I immediately wake up, that I will hear the answer, and I always do. The saying, *sleep on it*, are three words that always makes sense.

Dreams are wonderful insight into our inner being. To dream and remember that dream is one way messages are sent to us. Acknowledging your dreams can alter and improve your life in unimaginable ways. If you are stuck on something while awake, sleep and dreaming will sort out the problem. The answers are there. I believe that dreams hold a vast array of messages concerning all aspects of one's life. As you read some of the amazing dream stories in this book, you will understand why I believe we are sent messages from our Angels and Guides and how it is important to listen to them. You need to access your inner being and become open and aware of those gut feelings. Then you can ask for answers to be sent to you. But, who are you asking? I say this constantly, that we are born with protection and guidance.

As loved ones pass, they too watch over and make sure we are guided right. Most people mistrust their own instincts and inner guides and instead ask for advice from any and everyone around them. The influx of diverse opinions creates more confusion in finding answers. If you just allow yourself to quietly sleep, believe, open your heart and mind, trust yourself, trust your Angels, you will hear the messages and move forward toward your goals. When you feel something is wrong, it's usually wrong. When it feels right, it's usually right.

When your prayer is answered, or a dream sends a message, you must listen to it. Deep down, it is helping you to move forward. Whether it's a creative dream, a warning dream or a dream sorting out problems, they are all worth evaluating. They can provide you with answers and direction that can enrich and alter life as you know it. I pray for messages to come to me through my dreams. I ask people in my dreams questions and they answer. I am truly amazed by this and always talk about the dreams I have. I also happen to be clairvoyant. This means I see visions of future events that will usually occur. This is quite different from a dream message. The clairvoyant vision can flash in an instant while awake or sleeping. It can be a good or bad vision. In my life, everything crosses each other, prayer, dreams and psychic abilities. It took me some time to distinguish the different nuances. But, they are all quite unique and very much different.

Prayer for me is the most powerful way to ask and receive. My paranormal gifts and abilities to communicate with the other side are for guidance and messages. Dreams are the unconscious messages that will help your decision process before it is made in reality. You can decide what is or is not bothering you. Don't make any drastic decisions. When in doubt, sleep on it. Experiencing and witnessing the enormous value a dream holds, keeps me extremely aware and receptive. When you dream, it is important to search for the messages, especially if you are new at this. Once your awareness is heightened, the messages will come in very clear. You will want to dream and remember every one of them.

When SPIRITS speak…

I was dating this man for a few months. He really did not believe in Angels and the power of prayer. He listened to my stories, my dreams and my visions. Things would happen that I prayed for. My clairvoyant visions would happen. But he still doubted my spiritual strength and gifts. Nevertheless, I filled his ears with all my stories and said I would pray that he gets a message. He joked continuously that he hadn't received any messages other than his phone messages. I didn't get annoyed and just said, "One day, you will believe and you will see."

A few weeks went by until one night I went to sleep, prayed as usual and dozed off. I woke up after dreaming an incredible dream. In my dream I arrived at a party with a lot of people already there. I was hopping from person to person, talking to each and every one of them. I noticed a girl sitting on a chair in the corner of the room just watching everybody. She had dark hair in a bob cut, a little chubby but very pretty. She was very detailed, more than the other people in this dream. Next, I did what I would normally do in real life in my dream. I walked over to her and said, "Hi, my name is Gina." She replies, "I know, I'm Sal's sister." Sal was the man I was seeing. I recall him saying he had a sister that had passed away. I stared at her for a minute and asked, "Are you Marie?" She answers back with a stern tone, "My name is Maria." I say, "Ok, I'm sorry, I didn't know it was Maria." She says, "Please

tell my brother everything will be alright." I said, "Ok".
Then I woke up.

I immediately had to tell Sal this dream and message. I told
him the whole dream and described Maria to him exactly
the way she appeared to me. I had never seen a picture of
her. Tears started to roll down his face as he went into his
briefcase. He took out a photo of his sister and handed it to
me. He said, "She hated to be called Marie, and was always
correcting people in a nasty tone saying her name was
Maria."

I said, "That's her, that's really her. She was in my
dream." I stared at that photo for a long time. I described
her to perfection. I was amazed. Sal had tried to save
Maria's life, he donated his bone marrow for her, but it did
not work. He missed her very much. The message was for
him. Spirits and Angels know I will give the message to
anyone it's for. I don't care if people think I'm strange or
wacky. When I know the messages are for someone else, it
is amazing to see what that other person's response is when
I tell them. Sal's sister wanted him to believe. This was her
way to send a message and let him know she is watching.
He was shocked and confused, but now he was a believer.

On another day, I was laying down, resting before a poker
game. I had the television volume very low and just wanted
to relax. The person who was having the poker game was
someone I really didn't know. I had played poker with her

only a few times before, but we were becoming friends. As I lay on my couch, I hear a soft voice speak, "Tell Barbara I love and miss her and she still blows the biggest bubbles." Well, so much for my resting. I heard it again. I answered out loud, "Ok, I'll tell her." Now, I'm driving to the poker game that is at her house wondering how I was going to tell her this message. She is going to think I'm crazy. Nevertheless, I have to tell her.

I get there and a lot of people were there already. I can't tell her yet and I wait a while. We started the game and usually we break after two hours for ten minutes to eat and color up the poker chips. When it's time for the break, I took her aside and told her I was very psychic. She was so excited to hear that. I also told her that spirits speak to me and give me messages and that I had received a message for her. She was a little taken back and looked like she wasn't ready for all of this conversation during a poker game or any time. But, I said, "The message came in twice and it means nothing to me nor do I understand it. It is for you." She said, "What's the message?" I said, "The message is, I love and miss you and you still blow the biggest bubbles." Her jawed dropped and she ran upstairs crying. She did not come down for twenty minutes. The game resumed and I was playing, but wondering if she was alright. She eventually came back down and called me over to the side. I asked if she was ok and if she would share what that message meant. She said, "My best friend Randi died a week before my wedding, and I miss her so much. We always drove up and down the main street together chewing bazooka gum and seeing who could blow the biggest bubbles…and I always won. You don't even know me or anything about me, I am totally shocked and amazed". She hugged me and thanked me for telling her. We became best friends.

You may ask, what's the purpose of these messages? They really didn't guide them or answer a question, or did they? I believe when these messages are sent, the person receiving it is being validated. They are given this sign that they are watched and looked after. It should be taken with the utmost appreciation and realization that this information came from the other side to them and encourage them to believe in a higher power. Everything happens for a reason, every message is sent for a reason, and everyone always has a reason to pray.

Once you've decided to ask your Angels and guides for assistance before sleeping, you have started the process of pre-paving your life. You will want to elaborate what you need. Do you have questions that need to be answered? Did you prioritize your desire list? Let me give you an example of a list that I have done for one of my goals. Desire/Goal: I always wanted to play piano. This was stuck in my head for years. I learned the basics as a child and then gave up. Later in life, in my early twenties, it came back into my subconscious. I started to dream I was playing beautiful music. Awake, there was always an excuse not to; no time, too hard, too busy, etc. Subconsciously it remained in my brain. One day I woke up and heard that voice from afar say, "Today is the day. Look for a piano teacher." But before I did, I made a list.

1. Find an accomplished and strict instructor. Someone who will push me to practice and succeed.

2. Devote a minimum of two hours of practicing per day, for at least two years. I knew this is what it would take to accomplish my goals.

3. Let nothing distract or interrupt these two hours.

4. Pray for energy and determination to succeed.

5. Do not start unless your desire is strong enough to keep you focused on the goal.

Simple, huh? Not such a hard list. We live in a world today that is fast moving and with a 'got to have it now' attitude. Everyone wants everything with only having to do a minimal amount of work and putting in little effort and time. You need to detail and evaluate your desires so that you can attain them. Know what the time frame may be needed for you to accomplish it. Think about what it will take on a daily basis to stay focused and work toward it. The first excuse that pops up when wanting to play an instrument is it'll take too long and it's too much work. Well, the more difficult the goal, the longer it may take. If you dream or wish big, it is more likely that you will have to work harder and longer to get there. I tend to dream big and find myself always having those swings of high and low, waiting for results and needing to push harder after I'm already tired from the initial pushing. I am human like everyone else and I do have waves of uncertainty and doubt that I always have to fight through. I usually get sent a message or sign when I feel like doubt could be creeping in. I'll decipher my dreams and try to see the next step of action required. Prayer and meditation helps bring you back on track. Getting back to basics and appreciating all that has come into your life already helps you to move forward and regain strength.

I did what was on my list for learning the piano. I had many days that I wanted to quit. The studying got harder and the amount of practice required was enormous. I prayed and asked for strength to overcome some of the challenges and energy to continue. A day later, I felt this surge of energy and desire to practice harder. I became obsessed and crossed the midway mark. When you're past the halfway mark toward your goal, to quit then would be such a great disappointment. It is then when you need that extra strength to continue and finish. I did imagine myself playing piano so beautifully but felt I wasn't quite there yet. My mother was a concert pianist and played so beautifully. I just wanted to play and try to sound like her. It took a few more years, but one day my brother and sisters walked in the house while I was playing and thought it was our Mom. I felt a chill run through me and thought, "Thank you God for helping me do this."

It's funny the chain of events that follow a reached goal. My mother and I started teaching piano together and we held beautiful recitals at Snug Harbor. Our students were great and the experience of teaching piano was wonderful. During an extreme break-up with my boyfriend I had a dream of lyrics and music. It woke me up around 3:00am and I jumped up and went to the piano and wrote it all down. I went back to sleep only to keep hearing the melody and the words. I got up around 6:00am and continued writing it all down. When I play my song people have tears in their eyes and ask, "What's the name of that song and who sings it?" There is everything in that song that I was feeling and it came out through a creative dream.

Dreaming and meditation is the door opening to your soul and heart. It's a way messages come in from your Angels and Guides. You can find your path by spending time alone in that quiet inner world. You can find out answers to problems, make clearer decisions, get your life on track, analyze the symbols to help change your life and see future paths. Every dream has something in it that will have meaning to it. Whether it's a dream or a nightmare, you need to look deep into it and find the answers it is bringing to you.

CHAPTER 3

HOW TO ASK AND RECEIVE

How do you ask for something in prayer? Who are you asking? Who is listening? Meditation and prayer can and will change your life. It has changed mine to the extent that I now rely on prayer as the *first source* I go to. I have learned to prioritize my list and really know and understand what it is I am praying for. The prayers are not just a daily prayer to give thanks or to just ask for general help. I think about what I am going to pray for and the outcome that I want. It sounds easy, but, until you try it you won't understand how much effort is required in the details about what it is you want to pray for. Every little detail before the prayer needs to be thought out. It's your life or someone else's that you are praying for, so no detail should be overlooked. I believe it is extremely important to know exactly what you are praying for and why. I have prayed with doubt in my head and those prayers are never answered. When I know exactly what I am praying for the miracle happens.

Everyone prays for something at some point in their life. Many people pray without realizing they are doing it. Most people believe a prayer can be answered, right? Why else would you pray? I have always prayed and prayed for others. My routine prayer at night is:

> **Dear GOD** heavenly Father, maker of heaven and earth,
> My Angels and Spirit Guides...
> Thank you for everything you've given me...
> I pray for those who are sick and dying-please give them comfort....

And I believe in your healing powers…
Please keep the white light around me, my family,
friends, and my home.
Keep me healthy and positive and
I ask that you guide me and keep me on the right
path.
Amen

This is just my way of summing up in a prayer what is
good for me and what I need to express in a daily prayer.
Everyone should have a *personal daily prayer* for
themselves. This is an everyday prayer. Different from the
prayer you need to say when asking for something from the
LORD to give to you. I really think hard about what I want
to pray for concerning life's decisions. I want to be clear
and it needs to come from deep within the soul. The HOLY
BIBLE has great insight for us to use and we should
understand the power. On the subject of PRAYER:

> Ask, and it shall be given you; seek, and ye shall
> find; knock, and it shall be opened unto you:
> For every one that asketh receiveth; and he that
> seeketh findeth; and to him that knocketh it shall be
> opened. (Matthew 7:7,8)

> And all things, whatsoever ye shall ask in prayer,
> believing, ye shall receive. (Matthew 21:22)

> If ye abide in me, and my words abide in you, ye
> shall ask what ye will, and it shall be done unto you.
> (John 15:7)

> Therefore I say unto you, What things soever ye
> desire, when ye pray, believe that ye receive them,
> and ye shall have them. (Mark 11:24)

The Holy Bible has words to help us with anything we may need throughout life. There are so many roads we travel and stages we go through, that praying for what we need is according to each one that we may need help with. Some roads are smooth, going nice and peaceful, so just saying your daily prayer of thanks is enough. It's usually when obstacles appear and get in our way, or a marriage is failing, health issues arise, career problems, financial difficulties and so on, when we start praying hard. I have been through it all and I have prayed hard from my soul, with tears in my eyes. With a health issue, I begged for a miracle; to be healed and be healthy. I was given a new lease on life. I can't stress enough how wonderful it is to grasp the power of prayer, to pray to the LORD, to believe HE is listening and will take care of you, no matter what the outcome. It's important to *never lose faith* and to continue to pray, even when things do not seem fair. On the subject of FAITH:

> Now faith is the substance of things hoped for, the evidence of things not seen. (Hebrews 11:1)

> That Christ may dwell in your hearts by faith; that ye, being rooted and grounded in love, may be able to comprehend with all saints what is the breadth, and length, and depth, and height;
> And to know the love of Christ, which passeth knowledge, that ye might be filled with all the fullness of God. (Ephesians 3:17-19)

So, how to ask and get what you need? Well, I make a list of what I want to happen in my life, where I see myself regarding relationships, work and my well-being. Each area needs to be looked at closely and thought about. For instance, my career has been through a few ups and downs.

I am not as happy in it anymore and I am trying to revamp it. So, I put together a few ideas of what I want changed and make a list of what I need to do to initiate those changes. Along with that I pray and ask for help and guidance along the way, to be sent what I need to accomplish it and to be patient. I'll ask for it to happen within a certain time frame, and promise to work hard for that change. GOD helps those whose help themselves so making sure you are helping yourself and not just waiting around for gifts to be handed to you is vital.

When you are alone and frustrated, pray! Some say it is mind over matter, but really, praying and then watching things happen around you over and over again is not a coincidence and it will build your faith. It may take time to organize your thoughts and detail what you want to pray for.

So, try a little test of Faith. Spend one week writing down something you want, or want changed, or want to happen in your life. Be specific and detailed. Put that information on one side of a piece of paper. Try to visualize what you are praying for and imagine it happening. On the other side of that paper, write down WHY you want it and WHY you deserve it. Also, write down what you will do to work for that change as a sort of promise you will have to keep. Now, pray every day for it to happen. Be aware of signs, people and any type of message that may come your way. I have been floundering about a few things like moving, career change, personal issues and financial issues. I am not exactly sure about what I want to do yet, so I am not praying yet for any of these issues. I have tried and nothing happens. I am only sure right now about this book and that is what has taken precedence over anything else. I am confused on all other issues and I am just praying to be helped with the direction I should go in. I will wait for signs that will lead me to the right decision. Sometimes you have to sit back and wait. Eventually, the path looks clearer and decisions become easier.

Now that I have promised to finish this book by a certain date, I have to actually write almost every day to complete it. I always expect I will get what I pray for and it always comes. I pray to my Angels and my Spirit Guides and ask them to guard over me, keep me motivated, energized, healthy and have no distractions so I can concentrate on completing this book. I have the same difficulties as anyone else. I can wake up tired, not motivated, busy with other projects and distracted. So pray for what you need and include what you will need to help you appreciate and work towards the main thing you're praying for. After praying, I now wake up ready to write and could care less about anything else. This is really not usually how I am. I subconsciously made this my main priority and now that I only have a few chapters left, I am obsessed with finishing it. I am actually upset if I don't start writing by 9:00am. Obsession is a great quality to completing any project. It has to creep in your head and soul. Nothing should get in your way and you should be happy while in the process. There will always be some distractions, everyone's life is full of them, but staying obsessed and focused eliminates most of them.

I am still grieving my Mom and I feel her everyday around me. She sends messages and signs that are ever so comforting and as much as I miss her, I know how happy she is on the other side. Angels and Spirit Guides are listening. They will send you signs to help you on your way. It's very easy to go about your busy day and not give them even a moment of thought but they should be treated the same as if they were alive and called upon the same way. I used to call my Mom at least twice a day, so now that she has passed, I still speak to her at least the same if not more. I can communicate with her and she is watching over and guiding me. So, call upon them as much as you want. There can be times when you think no one is listening or nothing is happening, even then things are in motion. I too get impatient sometimes and want the successes and outcomes in my life to happen faster. I usually end up praying harder.

When I pray, the prayers are from deep within my soul. I actually can feel an energy within my body that I can't explain. I also get teary eyed and very emotional. These heartfelt prayers are always answered and rather quickly. It's important to pray from the heart and soul. You should feel love and a bonding moment with GOD that fills you with emotion. Over time you will become better at ignoring distractions and feeling connected more easily. When you pray like this and you experience that moment, you will feel something and you will now have learned how to really pray.

As I said before, sometimes you pray more at times of difficulties or when in a period of making changes. I have been praying constantly lately. This year has been challenging to say the least. Things are easing up and now I am in a career change. I have been a little confused of what path I should take and even though I am praying for guidance I am not receiving any strong signs of what to do. I know this is because I have some doubts and that is what is blocking my direction. I do keep hearing faint voices saying to slow down and just finish what I have started; take it slow, wait a few months. These are my Angels and Spirit Guides talking to me. The voices are soft and faint, but very clear. When I meditate, sit quietly and open my mind, family and friends that have passed appear and speak to me. I am so blessed to have this gift and to be able to connect with them. It is comforting to know they are there to watch over and let you know how present they really are. They are there to help guide you, so speak to them and ask for assistance.

These past years have been difficult for most people. We have been in a recession that is continuing much longer than most anticipated. These days most of us are concerned about the future, financial stability, health care and job security. It is time to work hard again and regain faith in what we can do. Praying, along with determination and hard work will get you to reach your goal. Pray for guidance and direction and you will see opportunities and doors open along the way. Choosing the right path and direction you want your life to go in will become clearer. I have been praying for guidance. I have quite a few projects in progress and it has been all work with no reward yet. Yes, I can get frustrated, impatient, anxious and even a little depressed along the way. This is when I pray, wait and listen for messages. Praying calms me down, slows me down and grounds me.

HOLY BIBLE GUIDANCE:

> A man's heart deviseth his way: but the LORD directeth his steps. (Proverbs 16:9)

> The steps of a good man are ordered by the LORD: and he delighteth in his way. (Psalms 37:23)

> In all thy ways acknowledge him, and he shall direct thy paths. (Proverbs 3:6)

> And thine ears shall hear a word behind thee, saying, This is the way, walk ye in it, when ye turn

to the right hand, and when ye turn to the left. (Isaiah 30:21)

So it's time to think hard about what you may want for your life and search deep in your soul. Since I had my scare with cancer and thought I may not live for another five years I now ask, what would really make me happy? How much work do I want to do? What type of work makes me happiest? What projects are going to be priority? You can get great answers after asking yourself these questions. Once *you know* what direction you want to take it's time to pray for assistance and guidance.

It's helpful to make a list of what you want to happen or what help you need and then make another list of why you want it and why you deserve it. Focus on one thing at a time and pray hard for it. Messages and signs can and do get sent right away. You just have to be open enough and alert. Recap each day and try to see what might have occurred during the day that may have been a message. We all are very busy and may not get the message right away when it appears.

I am in the middle of so many projects and drawn to all of them. I pray for guidance and to be shown which path is best for me to take. I ask for doors to open where I need to follow. Things do start to happen. I too need to take my own advice right now. I need to focus on one project and pray hard for what I want the outcome to be. Since I have many projects brewing it's important to slow down and decide which one needs more of my energy and work on it obsessively. When I pray for guidance I ask that any person that can help me be sent my way, any obstacles be removed, for positive signs to be sent and reinforcement and energy, always energy.

People that can help you will appear. Mostly unexpectedly when you're out or talking to a new friend. I believe people cross paths for reasons. We learn from each other, help one another and something is always taken with you that remains.

Asking and receiving comes in steps. Always really want what you ask for and be ready to work for it also. There are not too many handouts in life, but there are open doors and opportunities that will be sent your way. Don't get too anxious, some of the things we may be praying for take time. Some prayers are answered in a way that you may not like at the moment but will make sense down the road. I have a few projects that I have worked very hard for and all the praying right now seems to not to be getting answered to my liking. I tell myself that this is how it's supposed to go at the moment and there will be a reason for what seems like a setback. Yes, it's extremely frustrating to go through and I have yelled at my Angels and Spirit Guides, "WHY is this happening like this?" But, I have such faith in knowing that it all works out eventually and something will open the path for me to continue and move forward on. I am patient and I let things take their proper course. Everything just has to flow at the pace it needs. If too forced, it doesn't happen; if not enough effort, it doesn't happen. It just has to flow.

Being that I am clairvoyant, you might be wondering 'why can't she see where her own life is going?' It comes in waves for my own personal life and unless it's incredibly clear I can't see it. I am presently seeing glimpses of my future and it shows scenarios that I will be in. The timeframe is close because when I get these images, I know I am on the right path and that it will happen soon. I also start to get images and messages in my dreams and then the reality of it all begins shortly after. It's a wonderful experience to see these images and be excited to expect them happening in the future. I do see not-so-wonderful future images at times and as much as I wish them not to happen or try putting them aside, they always occur. I always pray and hope that I am seeing it all wrong and for the concerning images to go away. I saw my husband's death the night before it happened. I saw my mother's death and my Angels even told me the exact day it was going to happen and it did. I was able to get to her and hold her hand while she passed. I was recently driving on the parkway singing along with the radio and an image flashes through my mind and I saw myself very sad and teary eyed. I started thinking why would I see this and then the phone rang only to hear that my father passed away.

So, being clairvoyant is a blessing most of the time. I accept all that I see and can now handle all of the outcomes. Having a strong spiritual soul combined with psychic gifts has me on high alert at all times and open to what I need to see and follow.

Let's recap and list the steps for you to follow for heartfelt prayer and connection to God:

- Know *what* you want before praying for it
- Know *why* you want it and *why* you deserve
- Focus on one issue at a time and give it all your concentration
- Pray for energy and motivation to complete goals
- DETAIL list- details needs to be thought
- Pray from the soul
- Be patient and let things flow
- Keep eyes and ears open for messages and signs being sent
- Visualize your goals-see the finish line

- Work hard along with praying-there are no handouts

What I really want you to take from this chapter of *How to Ask and Receive,* is to not lose faith and be patient. To embrace the praying and the outcomes. To experience the wonderment when it happens and know when it is happening. You will feel so blessed when your signs and messages start coming to you. You may be in disbelief at first (like I was many years ago!) but so enlightened at the same time. Believe that your prayers will be answered and that you will contribute to whatever is necessary to achieve your goal. Believe and know that guidance and help from your Angels and Spirit Guides is always there for you.

Miracles do happen and in our fast paced society and techno world, we can miss a lot. Slow down and start to listen and look around a little bit more. You will be amazed at what you can see and hear. Open you mind to this process, ask for what you need or want, do the right things to help yourself along the way and wait for it all to happen.

Everyday life can always be full of excuses and get in the way of reaching goals. We all have and will have many similar issues to deal with throughout life. No road is without bumps and potholes. We drive on them every day and still get to where we need to go. Reaching goals, setting destinations and working toward getting to the finish line is the same as driving on the road, and takes as much practice as driving first does. We'll hit few potholes along the way and get aggravated, the roads get longer, more winding and busier. You must remember to stay calm, pray for some relief and a smoother path. I believe we all have the potential to pray and receive, believe in it, ask for it, work hard for it and enjoy the rewards.

CHAPTER 4

STAYING FOCUSED
(on Your Desires and Goals)

One of the most difficult things for people to do is to stay focused on a goal and to actually follow through to complete the work required to obtain it. How many projects have you started and thought, "What a great idea?!" How many have you finished? Do not blame yourself! You're not the only one at fault here since it's often made harder by our environment and support system (or lack of). We are not lucky enough to have things go smooth and easily every time. We have to clear the path of the obstacles one at time while staying focused. It seems funny that we all know what is in our way most of the time, but removing it seems too difficult. Make a list of all the things that may keep you from obtaining your goal. Here's an example:

1. Time
2. Money
3. My job
4. Confidence
5. Family stresses
6. Fear of failure
7. Resources
8. Bad experiences

First decide if reaching your goal makes it worth attacking the obstacles on your list. Something important to keep in mind is that whatever you put on that list could prevent you from achieving many things in your life, not just this one, if you do not come to peace with it or overcome it.

Do you want your desire enough to:

- Give less time to your spouse or children?
- To find the extra time and give up sleep time/work time/TV time?
- Save money for it; take from savings; give up other luxuries to be able to have the extra needed?
- Build your confidence and *only keep* a positive support team around you?
- Overcome the thought of failing and make sure it is something *you really can do?*

I found in this *Staying Focused* process that some of the people (family and friends) around you may not like that you are *not* giving them the attention they are used to and they're missing your company. Time taken away from those who want it from you will either help or hinder you. Scheduling your time is the best way. When I was studying piano, my practice hours were from 9:00pm-midnight, Monday-Friday, while Saturday and Sunday I had to block 3 hours straight and kept that flexible according to other obligations. My friends and family know when I'm in focus mode by my actions, and they also know now how to help me by asking if I need anything or any help with what I'm working on. And, YES, you will need help, so don't be afraid to request it kindly and then use whatever help you can get!

I *pray for energy* when working on a new goal. **Coffee works...*praying works even better*.** This is important for me because I never feel fully energized, even after a good night of sleep. Why can't I wake up raring to go? I dream a lot, wake up with thoughts running around my head and probably will never get the proper amount of sleep really needed to feel great. So, praying for energy *is* really what I need and always do. Every time I have prayed for energy, I have received an unusual energy and strength to work. It's totally a different feeling from your regular output of energy, as it should be, it's sent. I pray:

> Dear Lord,
> Please give me the energy I need to complete and fulfill my goals. I ask to have the energy I had when I was younger and I ask that no obstacles slow me down or get it my way. I will do the work needed so please send energy. Thank you dear Lord.

Believe it or not, when you have this greater energy emerge, you work differently. You get more done in less time and not only do you feel amazing while working, you start to gain the confidence knowing you can do what you set out to do. Along the way, I continue to pray and ask for anything else I need.

While you are working and staying focused it can seem like to others that you are being extremely selfish. Well, it's okay to be a little selfish about what you want and while working toward the goal. I suggest you tell anyone who may be unsupportive, jealous or interrupting your scheduled work time needs to either support you or just plain leave you alone. It has happened to me and I bark so loud that whoever is on the receiving end never bothers me again after it. You'll know who the obstacle people are. Get rid of them! They come to annoy and want to distract you from staying focused. They will sound something like this, telling you, "Take a break. You're wasting time on that How long are you going to be? Can you do that later?" All for the selfishness of their personal needs at the moment.

They want your attention and will try to get it. Do what you need to do, say what you must and stay focused.

Those that have witnessed my previous successes are the most supportive and look forward to celebrating when accomplishing each step. My friends are always there for me, supporting me, pushing me and praying with me. They ask me to pray for them and help them with the goals they want to achieve. We pray for each other and we want happiness for all.

While writing this chapter it has amused me that I was having the most trouble staying focused. A lot has happened, life changing events are occurring and I'm still trying to work on this chapter. I decided to pray for more energy and for my Angels to nudge me along. It was a long prayer asking for guidance and reassurance, energy and motivation. I heard a voice just say, two paragraphs a day. It was ever so soft and it hit me that yes, two paragraphs a day I definitely can write during this hectic part of my life. I felt an instant calm and relief that I could just slow down a bit but continue to work on my goal. In a world that revolves around high-speed internet, we need to remember that most of our ambitions and goals will take time and lots of it. So, pray for patience and stamina for the long haul and even if you can only give a small amount of time towards it, it's still better than no time.

I've been having a very busy month of extreme highs and lows. My energy level is also coming in waves and I haven't been feeling too good. I should be celebrating every night for the good things that are happening, but I'm not myself. I have aches and pains, headaches and stomach aches and no, it's not the flu. This is when it's very hard to stay motivated and focused. I started exercising more, walking the dog more, eating healthier and nothing is working. It all comes back to prayer for me. I prayed one night during this period and I asked to be healed and to please let me wake up feeling great and without these annoying aches. My prayer is from the deepest part of my soul. I usually get tears in my eyes when praying for something or even when thanking them on the other side for after I receive. I really count on the spirits and Angels on the other side. They are there for us and want to help us in every way. So after praying this extremely needed prayer, I fall asleep. I can only say this...*I woke up feeling amazing!* Not a single ache, I felt rested, I was energetic and I just yelled out "THANK YOU!" And you skeptics will say it's mind over matter. Not true, because I've tried that route many times. Praying has been my medicine for many things and only after a real prayer does this work anyway. I believe I was rewarded this for also taking it into my own hands and trying to eat and exercise right. When you reach a breaking point, Angels seem to know when it's enough. Pray and receive what you need.

Wow! This has been a stressful time for me and writing this chapter is definitely becoming memorable. I have had to pray the hardest I have ever had to in the past four weeks. My mother came to visit me from Arizona and usually stays for six weeks. I picked her up from the airport and the minute I saw her I was so happy and yet extremely upset for her health. She did not look well to me. Actually, she looked very ill and I felt a deep sadness and death around her. As she was staying with me she progressively got sicker and sicker, to the point where I felt she could die. I prayed she would get better, but it got worse. I'm now praying she doesn't die and I am trying to get her to the emergency room, but she won't go. I began calling my dad, brother and sisters to figure this out. My sister was yelling at me to call 911 and saying that if she dies it's my fault. All while my mother is yelling at me that she's not going to the emergency room. This was taking a toll on me. I looked up and said "Lord, help me, please." All of a sudden I burst out, "Mom, you have two choices. I am taking you to the ER today or you have to fly home immediately and go to your doctors there. That's it. Pick one now!" She chose to go back home. I sent her right away, praying she would not die on the plane; it was that serious. She made it home and they put her right in the hospital. The doctor said she could die within a day and needs immediate treatment. They found tumors on her brain pressing on areas that made her feel sick and emotionless. I prayed and sent her *all my Angels* to help her and that we were not ready to lose her. Crying every night and praying for any kind of recovery. The church held a healing mass for her. Everyone was praying for her. And IT HAPPENED. The Doctor couldn't believe it, but the treatment worked on her tumors and she slowly turned around. My Dad does not really believe the way I do and even he called to say it's a miracle and he has never witnessed this kind of turn around. The doctors are amazed and my mom sounds like her old self and is in treatment. This gives the entire family and my mother time to talk and say whatever needs to be said while she is feeling better, hopeful and in sound mind. We all know she is still very sick, but getting this time given to us is a beautiful gift from above. One month has passed, my mom had some hope and everyday got to speak with all of us. Slowly she is now regressing back to having the same symptoms. My dad has to take her back to the hospital and for a week she has been stabilized.

My brother Peter and I make plans around Thanksgiving to fly out to Arizona to visit with my Mom and family. My dad said not to come too early, she may think she is dying and that would make it more stressful for her. So, we told my Mom we will be there the week before Thanksgiving. It's October and I'm getting ready for bed on a Sunday night and I hear voices. Ever so soft they come and I hear, "Go to Arizona, your Mom is going to die Thursday or Friday". Well, it was clear and I was really scared. Monday morning I call my brother and tell him this and if he couldn't leave right away I was going without him. He said you're always right about this stuff I'm going too. We changed our flights and we called our family to tell them we were coming out. My sisters said that Sunday night Mom was getting worse and it was a good idea to come now. I told them about my message from the other side and they were just shocked about everything. At the hospital we all cared for and stayed with our Mother. My father and the rest of us were in the grieving process already. The nurses said it could take weeks and they are never sure how long it might be before she passes. Wednesday, October 23, she is very ill and spiraling down fast. I asked my Mom if she wanted to pray and she said yes. We prayed a lot that day and it's so terrible to watch someone in the dying process. Thursday comes and we are told once she is put on morphine she will not be able to talk anymore and will begin the process. We all spent the entire day with her, talking to her, kissing her and letting her know it was ok to leave us. I got to tell her that she was the best mom anyone could ever have and that I was thankful for all the wonderful things she taught me and for not only being my mom, but my best friend throughout my life. We as a family agreed it was time to let the nurses give her morphine and to let her go. Thursday evening she is put on full Morphine; we say our last goodbyes and Friday she dies while I was holding her hand.

In the hospital room I saw her father in light form picking her up as a little girl and putting her in a fishing boat. I tell my dad this and he said that's what they did when she was a little girl. I was at peace seeing this and sad to lose her but happy it didn't go on for weeks. The message was exact, her predicted death for Thursday or Friday was the message from the Angels and that's what happened. My sisters and brother cannot believe how I get these messages and they are always right. Thanks to the message I received we were all there for my Mom as she passed peacefully in her sleep.

I am so thankful to get these messages, for if I didn't I would have missed saying goodbye to my Mom and possibly missed being there to hold her hand through her passing. I am so connected to the other side that I could not live without hearing their voices. I will take a little time off from writing, and need to regain some new and positive energy.

So, here I sit after a short period of regrouping, finally without as many distractions to finish this chapter. I just really want to reiterate just how important just praying for energy can be. Our strongest bursts of energy are at the beginning of all projects and goals. Trust and believe me, pray for what you need, energy, support, financial relief or help from friends and family, receive it and use it. All you need to do now is work on what you want, enjoy praying for it and receiving all that gets sent to you to be successful!

I want everyone to understand that nothing is ever easy. Not for anyone. Some of your goals may be simple and easy to obtain and some very difficult with years of hard work to get there. I have been working on television production projects for four years now and one of them is close to getting aired. My family and friends must have said to me a thousand times that they can't believe I'm still working on these projects and always ask how I have the patience and stamina to persevere through it all. I always let them know that the big things take time and I have been sent everything I need in the steps that I needed them. Looking back over the past four years of working on two TV projects, it all makes sense. Each step and obstacle that I have overcome has led me to my destination. I absolutely look forward to everything that is on its way for me with excitement and enthusiasm. I am not afraid of hard work, long hours or giving up my social life. Staying focused when you can actually see the finish line and realize that your goals and ambitions are happening requires more energy than ever -along with a pat on the back.

When the goals and new life you are working toward are coming to fruition remember the process doesn't stop there! Look for those new signs and messages from above. They keep coming to help you through every phase. I will now ask for help to organize my life around a crazy busy schedule, to meet the right people I need for this new path, keep negativity out of my circle and to keep *me energized, creative and healthy.*

Staying focused to work on your goals is no easy task and to say the least can be extremely grueling, demanding of your time, energy, willpower and health. Ask family and friends for help along the way, pray for what you need and really need it or you won't get it. Spend a portion of every day working on your desires without interruption or negativity. *Weed out your life and keep the best around you!* Don't give up and pray for answers and messages for when the road gets harder. Whatever the outcome is for each step along the way, I promise you, that step was needed to be taken before getting to the next. I have cried and cried many nights wondering why something went the way it did and looking back, it was supposed to happen that way. I was extremely frustrated so many times that the tears would just well up in my eyes at any time. I didn't want to quit, but it had crossed my mind briefly at times and not without tears. I was moody and angry sometimes with my Angels and Spirit Guides. I have yelled at them to say I had enough and to stop making this so difficult. I remember that day clearly and I really couldn't take any more obstacles. I prayed very hard and relentlessly for an easy path of no obstacles and promised I'd work till I drop if necessary. My Prayers were answered! The obstacles have been small and too few to even mention and the pathway was cleared. I am enjoying the work involved for such a life changing adventure and the first television episode has been completed and I really can't believe how great it feels to get to this point.

Helpful tips for reaching your goals:

- Pick 4 days a week to schedule time slots to work on your goals
- Keep 2 days flexible and fit in some work on those 2 days
- Keep 1 day open for rest and relaxation
- SET GOALS for the Week/Month/Quarter/Year
- Set **Realistic** Goals
- **Pray for what you need** and look for the signs that are sent and use them
- Keep yourself motivated and focused
- Get obsessive –be driven and work hard
- Stay healthy and fit
- Depending on your goal…pace yourself if it's a hard one/have patience
- Lean on your family and friends-if they can help in any way-take it
- Cut Out the negative people and avoid them at all costs

Staying focused and completing what you have started is exhilarating. Don't be a talker, be a doer! Pick your goals wisely and go for them. Take your time, think through everything, plan, attack and pray! It will all come together and you will accomplish whatever it is you set out to do.

There are no get rich quick schemes, its hard work and one step at a time that will have you finishing the race. Enjoy the process and when over the peak of the mountain, pat yourself on the back, for it gets easier from then on. Keep a positive attitude and pray for energy, clear paths and anything you need to help you achieve your goal. Listen for those soft voices that creep in, act on them for they are your Angels guiding you.

I have become so dependent on my Angels and Spirit Guides. I will not go to sleep without asking them for guidance and to send messages and signs to keep me on the right path. It needs to be quiet and I need to listen right then when praying or I'll wake up to answers. Even when you are a little lost in what or where you want your life to be, that time space is important. I have been there a few times and not liking it at all, but, things happen in that period that put you on a new path or gets you organized again on the path you're already on. Setbacks are not really setbacks when you look back at them. It's all in the master plan and I want everyone to be able to see, hear and listen to what is sent for all to use to reach happiness here on Earth.

CHAPTER 5

LOSE THE FEAR

Definition of Fear: Feeling of anxiety, anticipation of danger, frightening thought.
Synonyms: Terror, dread, anxiety, horror, distress, fright, panic, alarm, trepidation, apprehension.

FEAR can cause certain physical reactions such as:
- Rapid Heart rate
- Increased Blood pressure
- Tightening of Muscles
- Sharpened or redirected senses
- Dilation of Pupils
- Increased Sweating

Small amounts of fear can be useful and serve a purpose-it can help you focus on a topic or task, so that you avoid failure. This type can sharpen your mind and senses which will help you achieve your goal. Another type of fear is the one that cripples you. Anxiety sets in, the not knowing is the worst kind of fear to experience.

People fear change. People fear failure and disappointment. Fear of changing jobs, fear of leaving a spouse and getting divorced, fear of raising children, fear is everywhere. Fear holds many people back from achieving their desires and reaching their full potential. Whatever the fear is that is holding you back from obtaining and succeeding what you want, needs to be removed. Most people do not trust themselves. We know this because it's commonplace for everyone to constantly seek advice from outside sources. Asking friends, family and just about anyone who will listen and give advice and assurance about your decision making may not be the best for you. Too many different opinions and options can leave you more confused and even more fearful.

Being less afraid of change can take time and be a gradual process. Going through the process one step and one goal at a time will make it easier to hurdle this. Asking your Angels and Spirit guides to assist you and help steer you will be most beneficial. Asking them for strength, courage and having a great desire for the change will have you on your way. *I believe in solitude, meditation and prayer for most decision making.* I listen to my Angels and Spirit Guides, I hear my own inner voice and ask for answers. I have learned to listen and do what I have to without fear or stress. Did something in your life just feel so perfect and you actually took a moment to catch the amazement of it? This is bliss, peace, happiness and a calmness that without fear involved you get to feel and enjoy.

I have encountered fear of many changes and have overcome them with results in my life I could have never obtained had I given into the fear and stayed stagnant. I also know it's not easy at all to say the least and literally having to grab your balls and dig deep to get through it takes all you got sometimes. This is when I pray and ask for advice and strength to do what I need to. If you pray strong enough from your soul, I promise you, you will feel a peace come over you that will calm you and help you through. I have felt this over and over and trust in it with my entire being.

I recall one night while in bed, a wave of fear come over me. I used to suffer from anxiety but, amazingly, I prayed for relief from it and has been dormant. I was making a career change and I was going through all my savings to do this. For me, anxiety turned into fear, usually when pushed to the limit that wave of fear can be felt. When it does, do you give in to it? Or do you say, I'm going to do this! My fear of not being able to pay my bills, not being successful in the transition, not making it was engulfing me physically and mentally. So, I do what I know best and works. I prayed for strength, a sign that I was on the right track and stay with it, courage and perseverance. I had tears in my eyes while praying and just asked for an inkling of a sign that it was going to be ok. The next day, I had a day to remember. I had received numerous calls for Artwork services. I couldn't believe it. They all hired me for work, and that was the start of my Art Business!

I have had many people around me witness my praying and receiving. They cannot believe how quick things change for me. Now, they are asking how to pray and believing in this. My Angels and Spirit Guides are always steering me in the right direction. Even if I don't like the path at the moment, I accept it, and go with the flow, because I know it is part of the journey. Years back, my husband had lost everything, my business was doing fine, but, I needed to carry the load. I prayed for work, and more work. I got busier and busier. My mother and sister used to call me a say, "How are you getting all this work through these bad times?" I answered, "I'm praying for it!" I was even astonished that I was beyond busy.

I feel I get sent what I need because they know on the other side that I will do what is expected of me. I feel this is a big part of getting what you need and want. You have to do the work that is required from receiving an answered prayer. This is no time to be lazy or procrastinate. Fear now subsides as the path gets clearer.

What are the most common fears? I can tell you from my own experience that there are a few that are overwhelming to get through, but every time I hurdled one, my life changed mostly for the better. There are a few big fears that most people will need to learn to face:

- Being alone: losing relationships through separation, moving, divorce
- Changing jobs or careers
- Moving
- Death: Spouse, parents, siblings, self
- Financial problems
- Health issues
- Not succeeding

It's terrible to say, but, experiencing these fears help you to have less fear as life moves forward. Once you have been through any of the above fears and have come through them, you are a changed and stronger person. I personally have experienced every one of the above and with prayer, faith and having great friends has helped me get through each scenario. The hardest and most fearful one is health issues, so after I experienced a major life or death health issue the rest got crossed off the list.

Being alone: I left a relationship at 27 and bought my own townhouse. Stayed alone for years, working on my career. I met someone who I wanted to marry and have at least one child with but, it didn't work out and was alone again. I didn't date for two years after that and never thought I could ever suffer from depression, but I did, and with support of my mother and close friends, an 8 month ordeal was tackled. I don't fear being alone…I may not like it or want it, but I definitely do not fear it anymore!

Changing jobs or Careers: I have done this quite a few times. With every move, I made more money and achieved more goals than I thought I could. Being in a new environment, adjusting, setting new goals, working harder to attain what you need and want for your desired life style, all comes from making wise career decisions. I look forward to new endeavors and I now get excited to see where and how far I can go.

Moving: I have moved so many times, in state, out-of-state, that I am a professional packer. I was living in house for 11 years with my husband and then had to sell it after he died and move to another state, downsizing my bills and household work load. I moved to a condo on the beach and wanted life to be easier. The move was extremely stressful, the purchase of the new condo, the closing of the old house and the move had to be done within 3 weeks. All my friends helped me pack and unpack. I could not have done it without them. You must ask for help when you know you need it. I moved alone to a beautiful luxury apartment. I cried a lot at night or in the shower, not having fear, but, now frustration of being alone again, and still grieving my husband's death. I prayed a lot more during this time than ever. I was even more psychic and clairvoyant than I had ever been.

Death: When someone we love dies, our own fear of mortality is awakened. If possible, you can change your life drastically at these times, realizing that life is short and that why wait attitude can trigger a new course for you. When my husband died, I was 48 years old. It was sudden and a shock. This is one of the top three biggest fears and life changing occurrences that anyone could ever go through. Your entire life is upside down, your job is on hold, your mental and physical health is at high risk for problems, daily life is extremely draining and adjusting to someone not being there is brutally cruel and heart wrenching. Waking up from the shock and reality creeping back in is painful to say the least. Years go by and you find yourself in a new place, new life and on a new course. Fear has been conquered and life is never the same.

You can push through and jump back into life, with new goals, different outlooks, with a strength inside you that you can't believe you even have to live again.

Financial Problems: Well, we all have had them. At least, 99 % of us. Money has been the cause of many problems. Whether you have lost a job, changed careers and it didn't work out, started a business and failed, had a successful business, but due to the economy it has slowed down or whatever has caused a substantial financial loss that has affected your life….it can be devastating. I have personally made it through my business slowing down due to the economy. I have been struggling just to stay even and for me that's been good enough. I do rely on prayer and ask for work to be sent along with my own efforts to boost more business. This has worked for me. When I pray for work it always comes my way. I really can't explain it. I pray, I ask, I receive.

Going back to basics when financial problems arise can really help. Get a second job, work longer hours and ask for help from friends and family and the good Lord. The effort you put into trying, when you do pray and ask for some relief-it usually is answered with some reward.
Those who just pray and think that's it…sorry to say…it may not come. So, going back to basics means hard work and making a really strong effort to have things work out.

Health Issues: Whether it's your own or someone close to you suffering or having to endure a health problem, anxiety and fear are present. No matter how hard you try to stay calm, you can't and won't until a few things happen.

1. The Doctor gives you some better news.
2. It's not as bad as it's presented and is controllable.
3. You have deep faith and can pray with belief to be healed/saved/or given strength to endure.

While working on this book, you have read already that my Mother passed away from cancer. I was again thrown into a whirlwind of stress due to my own health now. My stomach was hurting for a few days and then it got seriously distended. I KNEW something was wrong. I cleaned my house, organized a plan for my dog Romeo, packed a suitcase and walked myself into a hospital with my girlfriend Jill. My ex fiancé showed up and they both held my hand through every step. My brother then shows up and now I am in full panic and fear mode for my life.

I was put through every test and needed every one of them and then I was diagnosed with a tumor on my right ovary. All the tests were positive for Ovarian Cancer. I'm not going to lie or even soften how I felt. I immediately was in in shock, crying, automatic depression about how long I have to live set in and I did not want my family to suffer through this with me so soon after my Mother died, and I just wanted to go kill myself. I know it's against my faith to do so, but the thought was in my brain rattling around. Jill and Vincent (my Ex) made all the calls immediately to get me into Sloan-Kettering hospital in NYC. They took me the next day and they confirmed the tests.
I once before had a growth in my breast and all the tests were positive for cancer, but when I came out of surgery it wasn't. I asked the Doctor if that could happen again, and

he stated it's always a possibility but your situation now does not look to be so.

I am in shock now and it's actually sinking in what I may have to endure. I have never experienced fear to this extent before. This is a life and death fear! I felt I had no control over this and who do you turn to when this strikes you? GOD, Jesus, Mother Mary, prayer and faith is all you have. NO amount of money, no amount of good friends and family can ease the mental and physical suffering that you will have to bear. You are alone with the LORD.

As I lay in the waiting section for pre-op tests something happened. I saw and felt a white presence enter my body float around my tumor, weave around throughout my stomach and exit out my nose.

Now I have a few days before surgery and the next day my Aunt Mari comes to visit and I tell her what happened. She starts to get teary eyed and says my friend is very spiritual and sent you white light yesterday, don't know what time. I said it happened around 12:30pm. She called her friend and she sent it at 11:30am. I was amazed.

I'm in the waiting area at Sloan. There are many people in this section, all women who had ovarian cancer and they see me crying. A woman came up to me who was diagnosed with this and gives me hug and says it will be ok. She (Susan) states she has stage 4 and is still here 3 years later and feeling great. She then hands me a beautiful little glass bottle with Mother Mary in silver on it filled with Holy Water. She says take this, it has brought me luck. I immediately put some Holy Water on me and started hugging her and crying again. So thoughtful and beautiful.

My girlfriend Tasha on the day of the surgery at 5:00 am in the morning shows up at my door and hands me Rosary beads to take with me. I also took my mother's angel bracelet and the little bottle of Holy Water.

Now the day of the surgery before I go in and before I had any medications I start my prayers. Another wonderful happening occurs....I see my deceased Mom, Husband Sal and my Grandparents in light form and they are holding hands circling around me. As this is happening I see JESUS and I am so happy to see HIM and everyone else. A *peace comes over me* and I kiss Jesus's feet and ask for Him to walk in the operating room with me and heal me. In return I will make a difference, finish my book and follow wherever I am led.

During the surgery a prayer chain was started for me everywhere, New York, New Jersey, Florida....My ex-boyfriend went to a church, a synagogue and the hospital chapel. He prayed and cried his eyes out.

The MIRACLE happened, my Surgeon could not believe it and I was told he even went to pathology himself before closing me up to make sure it was benign. It was! It's incredibly rare and the team of physicians were all amazed. Some said I was blessed and I answered every time, "I WAS!"

The fear I had throughout this was unbearable. There is absolutely nothing from this day forth that can bother me or affect me negatively. Once you have experienced a health fear for your life, everything else is a walk in the park. I am so thankful for my miracle and for fear to be removed from my world. It will only open doors and put me on paths that will lead me to new wonders and adventures in life. I was already in progress for volunteer work for pet therapy for hospitals. My dog Romeo is ready and so am I. After I heal, I will be taking him to make someone sick happy, even if it's for a little while.

There is a saying, "You can only heal what you have suffered", well, I am thankful for all the situations I have endured for I am happier with the person I have become. I have been humbled. I feel and look at life so differently. It's so short our trip here to earth. Finding comfort, peace and contentment with all you have and not looking at what you don't have. Loving your job. Learning more. Teaching and passing on insight. Caring for family and friends. Enjoying your pets. It's all part of growing and living. I look at everyone and everything with new eyes.

The hospital had volunteers offering prayer periodically and I accepted a prayer every time. There was one prayer that brought tears to my eyes. It's a PRAYER for the SICK and a prayer to help with the fear.

Do not look forward to the changes and chances of this life in fear;
Rather look to them with full hope that, as they arise, GOD will deliver you out of them.
He has kept you your entire life…
Hold fast to his dear hand and he will lead you safely through all things –
And when you cannot stand, he will bear you in his arms…
Do not be afraid of what might happen tomorrow;
The same everlasting Father who cares for you today will take of you tomorrow and every day.
Either He will shield you from suffering or give you unfailing strength to bear it.
Be at peace then and put aside all anxious thoughts and imaginations that can scare you.

I know that all of us at some point during our journey in life, has similar situations that we all can relate to. The anxiety, stress and overwhelming fear it causes. Good fear and bad fear, whichever it is, always needs to be addressed and removed so that we can enjoy ourselves through life and work efficiently towards our goals. There has been nothing more productive and calming for me than to quietly pray and find the answers that are needed to remove all of this emotional chaos.

CHAPTER 6

DIVINATION TOOLS -SPIRIT BOARD

I admit; it's *amazing* and *terrifying* at the same time. Everyone at first is excited to see what will happen; hoping loved ones will speak and send messages. You have secrets and know personal information that only you hold inside. You doubt the board and have questions to test the validity of it. But, most of all, you believe in something, so curiosity brings you to a Ouija Board session.

I seldom use any divination tools. The Spirit board I also seldom use. But, when asked in the past I have and I usually partner with a psychic friend of mine whose name is Rose. If she is not available, I will ask someone who truly believes in the spirit world and ask if they would like to partner with me. We always have Ouija board sessions with a group of no more than ten people. A pen and paper is passed around and everyone is asked to write names of only the people they would like to speak with. This is done because I want only those on that list to come forward. Otherwise, other spirits tend to come in and disrupt the session. Sometimes these spirits are good and sometimes not, hence always asking only for those on the list. Also, someone is asked to write the letters and numbers that come up while receiving messages. The pointer can sometimes move very quickly and we call out letters too fast to put the words together, so someone needs to be keeping record. Then we can read the words spoken to us after the pointer stops.

Your heart races, the room gets silent and the prayer to open the board begins. After the prayer, the names on the list are read out loud and called upon to begin speaking through the board.

Ouija boards were first marketed in the 1890's. The word "*Ouija*" comes from the French word 'oui' and the German word 'ja', both meaning yes. You must have at least two people to use the Ouija board. It is said that if only one plays that a spirit might enter their body or the board won't work at all. The 'pointer' or 'planchette' is the device used that moves over the board with energy flowing through it which you have to experience to believe. If anyone has experienced the Ouija board they'll agree that it is *not a toy* and should be respected and used with caution. If used as a game, heed warning, you may leave the door open for dark spirits to come through and even worse they might stay to disrupt your life.

My Ouija board is blessed with Holy Water. I always open the Ouija board with a prayer and the lighting of three candles.

The *prayer is* as follows:

> In the name of the Father, Son and the Holy Ghost, please guide and stay with us while we ask to speak to those who are called upon. We only want to speak with good spirits. Allow only good spirits to come in and keep evil spirits out. We ask for: (read names off list)

What moves the pointer? Spirits move it through your energy. You feel their presence immediately and it is amazing to witness. My mother who was a little skeptical asked to participate with the pointer one session. She and I, barely touching the pointer with our fingers, watched it move over the letters. She was stunned and kept saying, "I can't believe this".

Ouija Board Story # 1

Rose and I are asked to have Ouija session. Six people come and I know only two of them. One man said he'll stay and watch, but didn't really believe in all of this, and came because his wife wanted him to. While I was getting the candles and matches, Rose got the board. We all gathered around and everyone seemed nervous. Rose opened board quickly and didn't pray. The room immediately got ice cold and both our noses start running. I yelled, "close the board!" She did and then starting praying while re-opening it. These people were already freaked out partly from me and Rose and because they were ice cold also. As quickly as the room got cold, it warmed back up. We now proceeded with the session. Spirits were coming in for everyone and it was going wonderfully. This one couple that did not believe in this, came just to watch and did not write any names on the list were riveted by the whole thing. Spirits were present for the others and they were amazed and exhilarated just watching. I turned to this couple and said, "Is there anyone you wish to speak with?" He responded quickly with, "You find out." I asked for any spirit that had something to say to them to please come forward. The pointer started to move fairly quickly. The writer started writing down all these letters that made no sense to us. It spelled, L-C-R-T-I-A. Then I asked the questions.

"Do you have a message?" It went to *YES*.
"What is your message?" It spelled, I-S-O-R-Y
"Are you happy on the other side?" It went to *NO*.

If a spirit is not happy on the other side this can mean a few things. One is that they are confused where they are or with what happened to them, a sudden death possibly, and the other possible reason is that they took their own life. I continued.

"Did you commit suicide?" YES
"How did you die?" This was crazy, it spelled, C-A-R, G-A-S, P-I-L-L-S.
"Did you try three times?" YES
"Was it pills, the third time?" YES
"Why did you do this?" B-A-B-Y
"Is the baby alive?" NO
"Was this your baby?" YES

Now, I am so involved with this that I haven't looked up at anyone. Rose and I are extremely focused on our questions and we too get mesmerized as it occurs because the information is meaningless to us and until we can verify what it all means, we just keep getting answers. But, I now feel the need to look up, because I hear nose blowing and sniffling. There was the couple crying and in fear. I asked if they wanted me to finish and they nodded yes, so I did.

"Your baby died?" YES
"Is that why you killed yourself?" YES, I-S-O-R-Y-S-O-R-Y-S-O-R-Y

I asked the couple if this made sense to them and if so to forgive her and say something to her. They had not spoken through this entire session. The woman said out loud, "We forgive you". They were extremely shocked and upset, and we asked them to explain. The husband could not even speak and ran out of the house so frightened, that we were all upset. The wife stayed at the table and explained;

> Our relative's name who killed herself was **Lucretia.**
> She tried three times to kill herself: exhaust from the *car*, **gas** from the oven and then with *pills.*
> She died from a pill overdose in a center for suicidal persons.
> She killed herself because she had killed her *baby*.

Ouija Board Story # 2

We had done a few Ouija Sessions in a row and every session the pointer would spell out T-O-M. This happened about three times in a row and I would speak out loud each time that there was no Tom written on our list nor does anyone here know or request a Tom. It was a few weeks later during a Ouija evening and again it keeps spelling T-O-M. I ask everyone to help me with this since it was now the fourth time this Tom spirit came upon us. I begin asking a few questions.

"How did you die?" The pointer keeps moving to the letter T, over and over. T-T-T-T

Everyone in the room is thinking and one lady yells out "Twin Towers!" and the pointer moves over *YES.* Understand that when operating a Ouija board any questions asked out loud will be answered.

> "Did you die in the twin towers?" *YES*
> "What was your job there?" F-R-E-M-A-N
> "You were a fireman?" *YES*

> "Where did you live?" Q-E-E-N-S-J-E-R-S-Y
> "You lived in Queens or New Jersey? YES-YES-YES
> "Are you kidding with me?" NO

Spirits will joke with you sometimes, so I had to ask that question. Everyone was now so involved in this and no one even knew a Tom. I now have to repeat a few questions to figure this out.

> "Tom, did you live in Queens and die in the World Trade Center as a fireman?" *YES*
> "Who lives in New Jersey?" It spells T-O-M

We pause for a few and I'm thinking...

> "Is there another Tom with us?" *YES*
> "Did you live in New Jersey?" *YES*
> "How did you die?" T-T-T-T

I voiced out loud, just out of bewilderment, "So, two Toms died in the world Trade Center?" It moves to *YES.*

> "Tom from New Jersey, what was your job?" F-M-A-N
> "So, you both were fireman, both of you are Tom?" *YES*
> "So, Tom from Queens, what firehouse were you in?" 1-3-2
> "Tom from New Jersey, what firehouse were you in?" 1-3-2
> "How many died from your firehouse?" 6

Now we are all intrigued. I really need to know what they want or they will keep coming into our Ouija sessions. Spirits know more than we do, so I listen.

> "Tom and Tom. There is no one here that knows you, do you have a message?" Nothing.
> "Please, we want to help, is there something you need to tell us?" Nothing.

Well, we finish our session and feel very bothered by these firemen. Everyone leaves and I call my girlfriend Nancy who is married to a fireman. I asked her if her husband was home and she said, "No, what's up?" I begin to tell her that our Ouija session was monopolized by two firemen that died in the World Trade Center and it spelled out the 132 firehouse. She was silent. Then she said, "That's my husband's firehouse!" I couldn't believe it. I ask her to find out about the people that may have died that day at the World Trade Center from his firehouse. She said she would get back to me.

Well, my phone rang very early the next day. It's Nancy. She said, "Bruce is really freaked out by this. Two Toms worked with him, one lived in Queens and no one knew the other lived in New Jersey(firemen have to live in the state they are employed), six people died from the 132. Two firemen named Tom were two of the six that died that day. He is in shock that you know all this." I said, "This makes sense now, they have a message for Bruce. That's who they want to speak with. They knew I would ask you about this. Tell Bruce he has to come and speak with them, it's very important, they keep coming into our sessions, he has to do this." She said he was too scared to.

Four months later, it's a hot summer day and Bruce and Nancy call to say they are coming over to the pool. I ask when we are outside relaxing if he was ready to speak with his spirit friends. He said, "Ok, I'm ready."

My mother was there and she and I opened the board. The two Toms immediately start speaking to us. The pointer was moving very quickly.

> M-O-V-E
> F-I-R-E
> N-O-W
> M-O-V-E

I continue, asking:

> "Move to where?" 1-5-7

I asked Bruce, "Bruce -is there a 157?" He nodded yes.

> "You want Bruce to move to the 157? *YES*
> "Is he in danger?" *YES*, M-V-E-N-O-W

Everyone is clearly rattled and the message is pretty strong. I looked over to Bruce and said, "This is a warning for you, you must listen to it. These spirits have gone to great lengths to get this message to you." He was terrified and amazed. He couldn't believe it, but had to believe it. He said he was thinking of moving to another firehouse and put in for a transfer. I replied, "The sooner the better." He did put in for a transfer and was just waiting for the approval.

A few weeks go by and Bruce got some type of flu and stayed home from work, which he never normally did. There was an extreme fire that day and his guys went in first. If Bruce was there, he would have been the lead man in. The first two firemen fell through the roof that day. His transfer led him to the 157. He clearly got a warning and was protected.

Ouija Board Story # 3

This particular session people are still talking about!! This was the first time this happened during a Ouija session and I was even shocked and amazed. We opened the board as usual, had the list of names and called upon them and the pointer began to move. My sister volunteered to assist with the pointer and the writer of the letters began jotting down what we called out.
We asked who was with us and would like to talk with us. It spells N-O-N-N-A.
I can't figure a word out and the pointer was moving fairly quickly over letter after letter.
All of us were confused except for one person. This one woman was Italian from Italy and it was her Grandmother who was speaking to her *in Italian.* We were so excited to see this and couldn't believe it. None of us spoke or knew Italian and to have the board speak to us in a foreign language was incredible.

Ouija Board Story # 4

One evening some family and friends were over and they asked me to do the Ouija board for them. So, we began, and two ladies did not really think it was for real and decided to test it.
My good friend stated that she wanted to see if we could bring in any spirits that would want to speak to her.
Instantly, the pointer began to move and it was one of her friends who had passed away a few years ago. The pointer was spelling out short phrases, miss you, love you, happy

here, still ok and so on. Then she asked, "Is anyone else with you?" It moved to *YES*.

She asked, "Who?" It spelled out B-A-B-Y "How Old?" 8-M-O. I looked over at her and she was crying. She says, "I need the name." The pointer spells C-H-R-I-S. My girlfriend almost passed out and had to leave the room for a few minutes. She came back in and said "No one could have ever known this. I had a baby that died at 8 months and his name was Chris." I was shocked that this came through, and shocked that she never told me this. She was a firm believer after this experience.

Ouija Board Story #5

This group of people at my Ouija session were believers, but still had some doubts. It seems that names and details in the messages from the spirit world is what really makes it valid to most people. My Mother, who after experiencing many sessions, was still slightly skeptical. I couldn't believe it when she said she needed a name to really be a 100% believer. Well, the board began to go crazy as if the spirits were annoyed with this group for still testing the spirit world. It spelled out N-A-M-E, N-A-M-E, O-K, H-E-L-E-N. My mother almost fell off the chair and that was the confirmation she needed. She never tested the board again. Another person said, "I believe in this because of all the information that comes through is so private and personal and no one knows any of this. But, if you can tell me what she was buried in, I'll never question it again." The pointer spells R-E-D-S-U-I-T, and his eyes began to well up with tears as he left the room. His sister *was* buried in her favorite *red suit*.

What is DIVINATION?
(From Latin *divinare*. To foresee, to be inspired by a God.)

The art or practice of trying to foretell the future or explore the unknown by occult means.

Religiously, we are brought up NOT to experiment or practice divination. There are a number of instances in the Bible that involve divining the future without any condemnations by God.
Some are: Genesis 44:5, Samuel 28:6, Numbers 27:21, Daniel 5:11. On the other hand, passages in the Bible that condemn divination techniques include: Exodus 22:18, Leviticus 19:26-26; 19:31; 20:6, Isaiah 8:19, Malachai 3:5 (and one of the most important passages), Deuteronomy 18:10-11.

The Ouija Board is deemed the most dangerous of the divination tools used. Why? The Ouija board is an open door for spirits and demonic spirits that try to come through. Repeated use can make the door harder to close. It has its own strange energy that moves the pointer and you can feel the spirits energy.

Is the Ouija board evil? No. It is like any other tool if the user is mature enough and respects and adheres to the rules of the Ouija board it is truly fascinating and enlightening. I seldom use the Ouija Board though, am still always nervous to use it and respect it immensely when I do. If misused, treated improperly or as a joke to conjure up or tempt evil spirits, it can be extremely dangerous.

Ouija Board Rules

They say the first rule is: DO NOT play with the Ouija Board but if you are going to, there are some major rules you must abide by:

1. NEVER play alone. Never.
2. PRAY before opening the board, ask only for good spirits to come forth, and those
only on your list that you want to speak with. Keep control of board and Spirits.
3. Accept no negative spirits.
4. Ask questions only with the right intentions.
5. ONLY one or two persons should ask questions.
6. Do NOT ask questions you don't want to know the answers to-example: "when will I die?"
7. One person writes letters down. Spirits might and often will misspell, use a different text style and even speak in
a different language.
8. Do NOT let the 'planchette' (pointer) count down numbers or alphabet. May mean a dark
Spirit is trying to come through.
9. Place a silver coin on board, it's known to repel darkness. (I light three candles.)
10. NEVER ask about GOD. (Belief is that Spirits that come through are considered evil)
11. CLOSE board properly, guide pointer down to the "goodbye" written at bottom of board.
12. Thank the spirits.

As a spiritualist and psychic medium, I do NOT need any divination tools to speak with spirit. Some do and enjoy tarot cards, tea cups, scrying, spirit boards, etc. that have been around for centuries. Most people who are intuitive or fascinated with the spirit world will dabble in one or more of these tools. Be careful and respectful and learn the proper way if you do. I don't recommend them and personally do not use them or the spirit board anymore.

CHAPTER 7

SPEAK TO THE OTHER SIDE

I speak to many spirits that have crossed over. I receive messages from them that help me with every aspect of life. These messages from the other side are to protect, guide, motivate, warn, comfort and help in the process of transforming your life. Messages and signs from the other side come in many different forms and ways. You may hear, see or feel something out of the norm. It may be a vision or a dream that helps you. It could be a new person you meet that delivers you a message or helps in your life transformation. Most people overlook some of these signs; even worse, see them and ignore them or chalk it up to coincidence when something does happen.

When you speak to your Angels and Spirit Guides you have acknowledged that they *are* there and listening, otherwise, why speak to them? Why speak to your Angels? They want you to succeed and they want your life to be wonderful and full of love. They will help you through the worst of times and keep guiding you through your entire life. Just speak to them and ask for what you need. I have no fear anymore of what life's journey may bring. We may not like some of what we endure here on earth, but knowing and feeling the presence of Angels and Spirit makes it easier and realizing the reason at some point why we had to go through what we did makes everything ok in the end. All of us have and will again go through periods of doubt and disappointments along the way. I sometimes quickly see the reason why something has happened in my life and the positive change it has had in my life. Sometimes, I don't see the reason for a very long time. I was in the process of a major career change and all was going great and then we hit a wall.

I am still waiting and wondering why I spent four years working on these projects that took an enormous amount of my time and energy to still have nothing come of it. During those four years there were extreme obstacles that I had to overcome to continue with the projects. I prayed very hard for everything to turn out great. I had many other people counting on me. They were excited for the opportunity I gave them, the life change to come, and to be a part of an exciting career.

They too put their heart and soul into the work and every step that took place, they were thankful and appreciative. We prayed all the time for the success of our new journey and to help us be the best we could be. We had the network, they signed us, we filmed, everyone involved were all extremely hard workers and nobody minded how hard we had to work for this. All was going perfect and then------out of the blue----we were at a full stop and to be put on hold indeterminately. A full year has passed and still nothing. I am human like everyone else and yes I cried, we all cried. I actually fell into a mild depression and so did some of the others involved. This was a real serious disappointment for all of us.

I did yell at my Angels and Spirit Guides over and over again. I am still upset and angry about all of this. I don't see the reason yet for why I had to do all this hard work to be led to a dead end pathway. I speak to Spirit on other side and continue to pray, but I am still waiting for some answers. Yes, you can yell at your Angels. In fact, I think it's a good sign back to them that you have had enough and are ready to listen and believe.

I know that there are reasons and it is for the good, why life's paths change or don't go well. I believe that we have to accept some of these detours and disappointments and turn it around. Yes, I am still upset and angry about why life is going array somewhat, but, I still believe the outcome will be for the best.

As you know there is Ouija chapter that tells all about speaking to the other side. I want to say I don't need the Ouija board to speak to the other side. Spirit speaks to me all the time. It's for others to see words spelled out by people who don't know anything about them. I may only use the Ouija board once or twice a year. It is not a game to be played around with and utmost care when opening and closing the board is a must! But, it works and is another form of communication with the other side.

I must say that I have had an extremely trying year and have been in a mild depression throughout. I feel that I am floating through time, a little numb to life and praying for some signs to come and show me a clear path of direction. I pray and speak to Spirit on the other side, begging for guidance and relief. One thing that I never lose is faith. Even through this entire year of chaos, deaths, career disappointments, relationship changes, family and health issues, I have maintained my faith. I believe when you speak to your Angels and spirit guides and let them know what you need in each situation that they are listening and will help you.

I always ask to be directed onto the right path I should take in my life. Even if the road seems a little winding and I may not be able to see around the bend, I'll trust in my Angels and continue on. I am on a winding road as I write this, but I am starting to see a little further down the road. Signs and people are getting sent to me every day that is bringing me back to a previous project that was put on hold. I call this the 'turn'. It's when things start to turn around. The 'turn' could be for good or bad. Knowing when the 'turn' is occurring is important. I'll thank God and my Angels and Spirit Guides that the 'turn' for the good is happening. They seem to know when you need it most. When the 'turn' is for the worse, I believe it's just something you have to experience and learn from. It's a side step that will help you get to a clearer path. All my 'turns' that I thought were terrible and unbearable, has made me stronger. I made it through those times and learned meaningful lessens. I was forced to make decisions that would change and better my life. Most of us will pray a lot when the 'turn' is for the worse. We start speaking to the other side all the time. Morning, noon and night. They hear you and will send signs for you to see a better way. The more you pray, the more at peace you will become with what you have to deal with.

Whether my life is going good or bad, I talk to my Angels and Spirit Guides all the time. I seldom put my radio on in my car. This is one of the best places to speak to the Lord, or whoever you wish that has crossed over or your Guardian Angels. Try it. Keep the radio off and zone in to the spirit world and see what happens.

I have asked and prayed for the most difficult things that others that have witnessed the outcome say; I really have an "in" on the other side. I was very sick two days before filming. It was the flu, but felt worse than any flu I had ever had before. The day before filming was to start my mother said I needed to go to the hospital that my flu symptoms were too extreme. I barely could open my eyes and told her if I go to the hospital they won't let me out. I have too many people counting on me for tomorrow and somehow I have to show up and do my part. She didn't think I would be able to. I started my prayer and asked, begged for even slight relief of my illness so that I can get through the long day of filming that I had to do. I cried while praying, saying that I had worked a year for this day and that I need one full day not to be sick for this. My mother heard me and said your prayers are usually answered, but you're really very sick and you may not be able to make it tomorrow. I replied; I am going to make it, don't know how yet, but I am. I prayed with tears in my eyes for any relief, took medicine, and went to sleep. I woke up at five am as if I was never sick. It was a miracle. My mother couldn't believe it. I worked filming all day and around seven pm I felt queasy again. I prayed again that I needed a little more time to stay well. I felt better. My last interview was at 1 am and I started getting extremely sick again. I was done filming and then was ill again like the day before. I prayed to get thru the day and that's what I received. I should have asked for two days of relief. The flu I had lasted for another two days. I asked, I received and I am always thankful. Being thankful on a daily basis is highly rewarded.

Whoever you pray to, ask them for help and guidance. Speak to them routinely and believe that they can and will help you from the other side. Have no doubt whatsoever and you will see things change. You can ask them to send you messages through your dreams, or through people who will cross your path, or whispered into your inner ear. I am not afraid, I look forward to hearing from them. Sometimes I feel like I am waiting a long time for a response, but usually it's fairly quick.

I believe most people have a slight fear of the spirit world. They may pray and believe, but really deep down have a fear of hearing a voice or actually seeing an apparition. I used to fear this also, not any more. I have seen apparitions, orbs, objects fly off tables and hear faint voices. Jesus has appeared to me three times in my life and I would love to see more of the spirits. Orbs are absolutely beautiful and mesmerizing. You can't take your eyes off of them. The light and love that I saw elude from it was beyond beautiful. I wish everyone could experience this at least once in their life. These appearances that occur in my life only strengthen my belief and bring me closer to the other side. I must acknowledge all of this and spread what I have witnessed. Giving hope to those who may need it and understand that spirit is among us and watching. They are here to help, believe and ask.

Whatever we're feeling, suffering or hoping for, speaking to the other side and praying brings us comfort. If belief is strong and prayer is from deep within the soul you'll experience a "knowing feeling" that all will be ok and whatever God has planned, you will be able to handle. If you are going through a rough period; never doubt what it is you may be going through, in fact, try to embrace it and reflect on the lesson it may be teaching you. Ponder the choices you may have to make to change things around. Think in a quiet place about what it is you need to do. Pray for help, answers and guidance. You can't hear the messages when distractions are everywhere. Keep TV's and radios off. In the silence comes loud and clear messages. Try it.

It can get frustrating when you are speaking to the other side and you feel like no messages are coming through. The messages are usually there, but we somehow can't see them yet. I have been going through this for a few months now. I have been confused on a few issues. The reason the messages aren't clear to me yet is because I'm not clear on what I'm asking for. The one message I received loud and clear was to sit and wait and be patient. I deep down strongly believe things go the way are intended, but I also believe that we have the ability to move things along and to put in the time and energy required to make happen whatever it is we are seeking. I actually don't make too many decisions without listening to the voices from the other side guiding my direction. If you are stuck on a decision, example; like whether to move or not, sit quietly speak to your Angels and ask for direction. It may come quick within that day or maybe days later, but you will get an answer. You will know when it comes to you. I am having this dilemma and what I did was just told a few realtors that I would consider selling if they had a buyer, but I'm not going to list my house. I don't have the pressure of listing and showing and I do have time to sit and wait.

You need to be diligent on speaking to your Angels. I speak to them every day. They see and hear everything. They are listening to you. Sometimes we have to trust how things are going and let them guide your steps. When you are fully absorbed by this and believe with all your heart and soul, there is a peace inside you that is such an amazing feeling. I used to have panic and anxiety attacks over everything. Learning and living by a strong spiritual faith has given me this peace. I am blessed to experience all that I have and to have no choice but to believe. I want everyone to experience this peace. Life is different living with Angels and spirit guides by your side. I know they are always there. It is comforting to have that overwhelming "knowing" and feeling they are watching and guiding. I am human like everyone else and get depressed and disappointed and fed up. Some things we must experience and just go through to get to the real finish line. I don't like some of these detours and setbacks. I absolutely have felt defeated and depressed at times. I pray more and rely on the other side to help me.

Just the other night, I went to bed and prayed to get a visit from anyone from the other side to come visit me. Whether in my dreams or awake, I just wanted to see someone. My mom, my husband, my friends, Jesus. Well, my husband

Sal came to me that night. I saw him younger and all in white. He held my hand and walked me through moments in our life. He spoke to me but never moved his lips. He also never looked directly at me; I thought that was odd. I woke up in the middle of the night and was so happy. As I dozed off again and he was there again. I said to him, I can't believe your still here. He said, I can stay with you all night. So he did. It was so beautiful to be with him.

Then one day that week I was driving to work and I saw a woman that looked like my mother on the side of the road. As I passed, I quickly looked in the rear view mirror and no one was there. I slowed down and turned my head to see if anyone was walking or still there and nothing. I believe it was my Mom. These sightings still amaze me. I love to see loved ones that have passed on and wish they would appear to me every day. I believe they appear to let us to know they are watching and that things will be ok.

I speak to spirit every day. It is now just a part of my conversation all times of the day. Lately, I've been blessed to hear voices from the other side direct my life. I first prayed that I get direction and help because I have been depressed and weak from grief and illness combined for over a year now. I felt completely lost and misdirected. So, of course, I pray for what I need. Then one night as I lay watching TV, I hear a faint voice say, you have to move. Listen now. I was thinking about moving but really wasn't ready yet. The next day, all day I kept hearing was this voice. Jeez, I say out loud, ok I get the message. I call a friend who is a realtor and tell her I want to list my condo. Friends were advising me to wait another month or two. I always listen to my spirit guides. My condo goes on the market and in two days it sold in the worst month of the year; January.

After listening to the Angels and Spirit Guides there is a euphoric feeling that melts over you. I spoke to the other side. I asked for help. I was answered with voice. I listened and followed through. I now feel wonderful about the decision which confirms how right it was. This is why I speak to the other side and wait for answers. I know it sounds crazy, but it has never failed me. Only the few times that I have not listened, I failed myself.

I believe everyone believes in something. Loved ones die every day and we go visit them at the cemetery, we light candles for them, we speak to them, we seek mediums to speak with them, we will do anything to speak with them…so is it so crazy to hear a voice or get messages sent to us? Of course they want to hear from us and help us.

I was praying one day to my mom who passed and to my husband who also passed. I asked for protection, strength and spirit back in my soul. I was dragging, drained, distressed, depressed and felt like my spirit for life had died off. I needed to bounce back and regroup. I needed an intervention. I went to sleep and had a wonderful vision. I say vision because the word dream doesn't encompass what I saw. There was a man in the distance with crowds of people wanting to see him. I pushed my way through the crowd and ducked under a roped off area. I looked up at the man and it was Jesus.
He was mesmerizing to look at. His eyes were a clear blue color of its own hue and it look like crushed diamonds were inside them. They were so beautiful and I stared right into them. I asked to touch him and he reached out his hand. I would follow him anywhere. He said he had to leave and then held up a cross to me and vanished. I woke up a different person. As if I was reborn. I feel so blessed to have had this happen to me. My life has turned around for the positive since then also.

111

Speaking to the other side and trusting the messages that come along is a key component to my existence. My clairvoyance gift has been stronger and I believe I have these gifts to not only help myself but others. I am obsessed with getting people to pray in their own way and trust in Angels and Spirits. Let them in your life, listen to the messages, you'll hear them when it's quiet. Feel safe knowing you can count on them.

I am so comforted knowing all of this. I am so at peace with life in general. I never lost faith through some of the worst times I have ever experienced and I am being blessed again and again. I can feel spirits in a room and I thank them for watching over. Those inner voices are messages and you have to listen to them. I look forward to speaking to my loved ones and acknowledging their life and the good they left behind. My mother taught me how to play the piano and since she has passed, I feel her in me when I play. I'm actually playing different, more delicate and beautiful and with her knowledge in me.

Love your loved ones with open eyes and open hearts. As we experience losing them, the more we will want to speak to the other side. I still would give up ten years of my life to have my mother and husband back on earth for one day, but their visits are confirmation that we go on and they are now my Spirit Guides. We all have Spirit Guides and Angels even if you don't know who they are yet. They are there and try talking to them. Ask for what you need and see what happens.

I want everyone to not be afraid of the unknown world of the dead. Let your loved ones back in your life, keep them close, talk to them and feel safe knowing they are there for you. I would love for everyone to experience seeing an apparition or to have Jesus appear to them. All I have witnessed and experienced gives me no choice but to believe. I can only tell you what has occurred. All my experiences have been beautiful and exhilarating, there is nothing to fear.

After getting through a really long and hard time in my life, I am now finding happiness again. This happiness is within me. The knowledge I have received through the tumultuous years and been enormous. The suffering, depression and emptiness I had made me closer to my faith and I was more so in contact with Spirit. The Lord has never let me down. My Angels and Spirit Guides have always spoken to me and guided me. I am a different person now. I am a better and kinder person. I feel more sympathy and empathy. I now feel and see more than ever with my clairvoyance gift. I could never go a day without speaking to Spirit. When I meet new people, eventually their loved ones show up for me to give a message. I feel balanced, blessed and calm. No amount of money can buy you this. You have to seek from within and from the other side. There is not enough time to waste time.

CHAPTER 8

PRAYING and BELIEVING

All walks of life have prayers that are unique yet still based on the same principles.

Let me start with an excerpt from one of my favorite little books, "The Art of Worldly Wisdom" by Balthasar Gracian.

> # 167-KNOW HOW TO RELY ON YOURSELF. In great crisis there is no better companion than a bold heart, and if it becomes weak it must be strengthened from neighboring parts. Worries die away for the person who asserts himself. One must not surrender to misfortune or else it would become intolerable. Many people do not help themselves in their troubles and double their weight by not knowing how to bear them. He that knows himself knows how to strengthen his weakness, and the wise person conquers everything, even the stars in their courses.

From the Bible:

> And all things, whatsoever ye shall ask in prayer, believing, ye shall receive. (Matthew 21:22)

I have had so many prayers answered that I cannot do without praying on a daily basis. Not only have my own prayers been answered, but my prayers for others also have been received. I wish for everyone to experience this to the fullest. The things that were most important that I have prayed for, I have received. On the other hand, some of my prayers that weren't answered yet may still come or they are not what I really need. At that crossroad you then have to accept whatever the outcome is, for acceptance and keeping faith brings you to another level. You are now calm and free to accept change and start different journeys. I was blessed last year with the gift of life and good health after my serious cancer scare and extreme surgery. Jesus appeared to me and I prayed for healing. Hundreds of people at church prayed for me and I was granted a miracle. The surgeon couldn't believe it either. He said I was under ½% chance that the outcome would be I had no cancer in me. He left me on the operating table to go to pathology himself because he said the results must be a mistake. My prayer that day was unlike any other prayer I have said. I begged for a healing and said I was the wrong person to give this to for I would probably commit a terrible sin of killing myself in the months to come. I promised to see life differently and help those that I could. I could not bear this illness and the other side knew that. Before surgery and before any drugs, my mom appeared to me along with Jesus and I felt they were watching over me but getting that healing miracle was just overwhelming and then I knew I still had something left here to do on earth.

Praying and believing is extremely powerful. When you get answered, it is sometimes a real surprise. I have prayed for things and the next day it would happen while I would have been happy if it happened within a month. I believe I will always get sent what I need, and what I don't need I don't get. This is important to understand but I believe the hardest to rationalize. Example: I met a wonderful man and we started dating. Everything absolutely clicked and was like a beautiful love whirlwind for five months. Future events and trips were planned in the holiday months to come and then one day out of the blue he says he needs space to find himself. Am I upset with my Angels and this abrupt break up? Of Course I am! I can't seem to rationalize what happened and why yet. But, I do know I have to believe in the path that is set and sit back and wait. I have to accept whatever the outcome is. The reasons why things happen and go one way or another *will* eventually be known. This understanding is what helps keep you balanced and sane through many rough roads. I'm human and did have a few bad days of being sad and down, but knowing what I know limits that to a minimum. Now I wait and continue with my life equally as happy. This too is important. You cannot put your happiness to be given or controlled by others. You certainly *can* let others bring more happiness to you and your life but, never depending on others for this. Only you must make your life whole and complete. Being happy within yourself and with your own world, you have created. Believing in your connection with GOD and Angels will keep you balanced and happy.

If you're wondering why you pray and you haven't received yet, there may be missing components to what you are asking. Also, you have to really want what it is that you are praying for; know why you want it, and why you deserve it. You also have to rely on yourself to work towards the changes you want. As I have said before, you may not receive what is really not good for you or for your future.

For instance; relationships. You may want to start dating again, but can't leave who you're with. You ask in prayer for someone to come along and help make the decision easier. It sometimes can be that easy, but it usually requires some work on our part before a prayer works. You have to leave the relationship that is not working, show strength and take the step that you can move on regardless. That shows how serious you are about changing your life and then praying for help and the guidance will follow. That is the step that I have realized over and over again. You have to be an active participant in your own life. I would listen to my Angels guiding me and do what I was told to do even if everyone else is telling me something different. The other side has never let me down. The outcomes have always been for the best and opened new paths that have been wonderful and exciting. I have moved three times based on hearing a voice saying it's time to move. Each move has been for the best and had positioned me to be in a better environment; emotionally, financially and physically.

With prayer comes strength like you have never had. Knowing you can get answers and guidance is a real ace up your sleeve. It keeps you balanced in thought and free from stress. Other than a serious illness, there is nothing else to really stress about. It's all fixable; money, work, relationships, etc.
I even believe in the miracle of healing illness. I personally have been miraculously healed and have felt the white light circle inside me. I have prayed over others and channeled the healing powers of the LORD through to them with wonderful outcomes. So with prayer and true belief that we are protected, we can move forward and ask for help throughout our life's journey.

Keep your home quiet and you will hear messages loud and clear. Pray from deep within your soul. Envision the Lord, ask for him to show himself to you. Embrace light and positive energy. Imagine a circle of light all around you and you're inside of it with GOD. Alone and in deep prayer. You should almost be in a trance like state of mind. Now really ask for what you need to make your life or situation better. Most times when praying my eyes well up and I get an overwhelming feeling of love. I also feel very safe and calm. I usually say:

> I will do what you ask of me Lord, please tell me or guide me on what do. Give me strength to actually do what you ask. Please send me what I need to get to where I want and need to be. Please help me to _____ (whatever it is your working on or need) and I will do the hard work required happily. Thank you for all that you have given me.

There are so many excerpts from the Bible about prayer. Here are a few I've selected that have spoken to me and impacted me:

> Ask, and it shall be given you; and ye shall find; knock, and it shall be opened unto you:
> For everyone that asketh receiveth; and he that seeketh findeth; and to him that knocked it shall be opened. (Matthew 7:7,8)

> And this is the confidence that we have in him, that, if we ask any thing according to his will, he heareth us: And if we know that he hear us, whatsoever we ask, we know that we have the petitions that we desired of him. (1 John 5:14,15)

> Thou shalt make thy prayer unto him, and he shall hear thee. (Job 22:27)

> If ye abide in me, and my words abide in you, ye shall ask what ye will, and it shall be done unto you. (John 15:7)

Along my spiritual journey I met someone who taught me a healing prayer. I had an ulcer pain while on vacation and really felt terrible. He saw me rubbing my stomach and walked over to me and said, "Let me lay my hands on you and pray for healing, you will be fine very quickly. If you believe." I replied, "I am very spiritual and believe in healing powers, but this pain takes two to three days to really subside. But I'll give it try if you say you can do this."

He lay his hands upon me and prayed in Spanish. Then drew with his thumb the sign of the cross three times over the area with pain. He then went back to his chair to leave me alone. If I tell you within ten minutes the pain was totally gone as if I never had it. Usually, I wouldn't be able to eat for days and the soreness would be there for days also. But not this day; I was healed. I walked over to him and asked what he said in prayer because I wanted to be able to do this not only for myself but for others too.

He told me the prayer.

> Dear Lord, God our Father, maker of heaven and earth. Please heal from the inside outside, cleanse the area of evil. Goodness in, evil out, goodness in, evil out, goodness in, evil out." To be said while making the sign of the cross three times.

I have done this many times since through the years and it has always worked. I have done this for others and it has always worked.

Sickness is a terrible fate. Bible excerpts show that the power of prayer for healing has been witnessed by many and there are unbelievable miracles.

For I will restore health unto thee, and I will heal thee of thy wounds, saith the LORD. (Jeremiah 30:17)

Heal me, O LORD, and I shall be healed; save me, and I shall be saved; for thou art my praise. (Jeremiah 17:14)

Keep your faith strong and always keep GOD close to you. Praying and speaking to him wherever and whenever you need to. Ask for good things to come your way and believe they will. Everything works itself out on its own time frame. We don't have the power to speed things up nor slow things down, we only think we do. *Just give in to what will be*. Work hard and relax at the same time and watch your world develop.

Try it for yourself! Here is my prayer for myself:

Dear LORD GOD heavenly father, maker of heaven and earth. Thank you for all that you have given me. Thank you for healing me. Give me strength to do what you ask of me and to make my life better. Please send me what I need- I need (ask for what you need in detail and then state why you need it). Thank you again for helping me and guiding me. Keep me healthy and strong. My Angels and Loved ones, please watch over me and protect me. I love you. Amen.

My prayer for others:

Dear LORD GOD heavenly father, maker of heaven and earth. Please help all the sick and the dying and send a wave of peace over them. Watch over my family and friends and keep the white light around them. I am praying today for my friend (name) who needs your presence. Please help them heal and send them what they need. Thank you for all that you have given us. Keep us healthy and strong. Amen.

I feel praying is really just speaking to GOD, Angels and Spirit Guides. I have full blown conversations with them. I love speaking to the other side. I love even more when they send me a sign that they are present through visions, scent, or better yet, when they show themselves. It doesn't happen often that I see a spirit form, but I always seem to want to see more when I do.

My hope for everyone who reads this that they are inspired to pray just a little bit more and a little different. Praying and knowing what you are praying for and why you are praying for it and deserving it to be answered all has to be covered. When you really want something to happen or change you need to pray from the heart and soul. You should get emotional and feel something different within you. Extraordinary events usually follow. All of a sudden you're in the changing process and you don't even know how it happened.

In silence you can hear wonderful direction. When you feel lost in life from stress, relationship troubles, financial worries, career decisions or health issues that is when most need to and start praying for something to give. Believing that the best outcome will eventually happen, knowing some suffering and disappointment will have to be tolerated along the way will keep you strong. We all get through life's turmoil somehow. There was a ten year period in my life that was just brutal. The first year I said, "Oh, it's a bad year." The second year, I thought, "Jeez, it's another bad year." The third year, I started stressing out and became very anxious about everything that was happening. The fourth year, I started having panic attacks. All along, I've prayed, but for some reason, things just kept getting worse. A friend of mine was going through troubles at the same time and she said to me she's not praying anymore. I fought her hard on this and said don't lose faith, we are supposed to go through this. It is easy to give up on belief when tough times last so long. The fifth year was brutal, my husband died suddenly. I'm in my forties, devastated and the grief seems unbearable. The sixth year, a transition year, moving and downsizing alone. Loss of work these years added to the stress. The seventh and eighth years were the worst. My Mother died, my biological father died and I was getting sick myself. I went through major surgery and a serious cancer scare of 3-5 years left to live put me over the edge. My MIRACLE came when I prayed for a healing as you read earlier. Life has been peaceful and basically getting back on course.

I moved again, met new friends, dated new people, fell in love again and started to working on my projects again. I feel like my old self which took years to get to again. I actually cried while thanking God and my Angels for this round of happiness and peace. It's so much more appreciated and not taken for granted. Whether my new love works out or my projects succeed, I will still be happy and thankful that I am not sick and in a really good place after all these years of grief and sorrow.

Once you have suffered a lot of loss and/or illness, everything else seems so simple to overcome. It's amazing how different you feel and how you see the world, family, friends, work and even your pets. I look at my dog, Romeo, with such enormous love. His spirit is beyond beautiful to me. I can look at my nieces and nephews and get teary eyed while seeking their soul. Look in people's eyes deeply, something will always seem different when doing that. The spiritual connection occurs or deepens.

My hope for everyone who reads this that they are inspired to pray just a little bit more and little different. Praying and knowing what you are praying for and why you are praying for it and deserving it to be answered all has to be covered. When you really want something to happen or change you need to pray from the heart and soul. You should get emotional and feel something different within you. Extraordinary events usually follow. All of a sudden you're in the changing process and you don't even know how it happened. I ask myself often, how did I get to where I am. It may sound crazy, but Angels guide you and when you listen to them and only them, it's always the right path. The peacefulness in believing in Spirit and Angels is beyond anything I can describe. It's a knowing that all will be ok and directing you to be where you are supposed to be in life.

Praying and believing that you can ask and receive will set your life in such a positive motion that you will not be able to not speak to the other side on a daily basis. Have patience and let them do the work and keep yourself aware of your surroundings to signs for you to absorb. I am presently in waiting mode for a few things. I am not dwelling on it, but I think about what I want on a daily basis. I put it out into the universe and in my Angels hands. I know the change is coming and waiting patiently for the transition is the hardest. We all want things to happen quickly. Sometimes they do, but most of the time they don't. In the meantime, stay focused and positive and continue to work toward your goals and happiness.

Life is constant change. I only recently have become truly aware of this to the fullest and felt that looking back in time or wanting an old life back is using up good energy for nothing to be gained in the end. Come to terms with this and continue to always change and move ahead. New friends, new places and new journeys are forthcoming. Praying and believing will help you get there and beautiful surprises will amaze you.

Chapter 9

SEEING IS BELIEVING

I have quite a few interesting stories about my clairvoyant gift and visions. My first experience of having this gift was when I was nine years old. I was playing with my dolls and talking to them about what was going to happen to me in my future. I spoke of meeting a man from Europe, travelling there when I turned twenty-one and never cooking or cleaning. My mother was listening to me and asked, "How do you know this will happen to you?" I answered, "I just know." She said that when I got older I would have to cook and clean and that is part of taking care of a home. I replied, "Well, I won't have to." She also asked how I was going to meet this man and I told her he would come to me.

Years later in my third year of college, I get a part time job at a restaurant. I meet a man from Italy who is a chef. We started dating and he took me to Italy for vacation. We got engaged, I seldom cooked and he had a cleaning girl. My mother said, do you remember what you told me as a child. I said yes of course I do and just laughed.

When I was in college my clairvoyant gifts were just starting to kick in. One night I dreamt of people in school talking to me and saying things that didn't make sense but it was what seemed to be normal conversation. The first part of this clairvoyant dream was me walking to the train. The wooded shortcut I usually take when running late for school had a spirit at the beginning of the walkway. It stopped me and said do not take the shortcut today. I listened and went around and heard kids fighting as I walked around. The rest of the dream was friends at school and instructors talking back and forth. This didn't really make any sense when I woke up.

The next morning I was running late and got to the shortcut pathway in the woods. I remembered the vision and heard the voice say go around. I knew if I went around I would probably miss the train, but I did and heard the real fighting going on the woods. Now, this entire day went exactly how I dreamt it from start to finish. By the end of the day I was floored by the events and having the gift of being clairvoyant. It was scary to me and I needed to try and understand it. It also was what started the honing of my listening skills.

The visions began to flood in on a regular basis. I would see a vision of a person or hear conversations and then within days the exact vision would occur. I didn't know why this was happening or for what reason I had been given this gift. Also, I had no one to talk to about this. A few years had gone by and finally I just start telling my family and friends these visions. I now wanted witnesses to what was happening.

I can see illness and death also which feels terrible. Sometimes I try to avoid it, but it happens anyway. Eight months before my husband died, I saw red circle on the concrete near the pool grounds in Florida. That was the spot he died in. I had it blessed. Soon after, I saw the most beautiful orb in the middle of the day hover over my deck off my master bedroom. It just floated in the air as if it were just looking at me and then moved towards me getting brighter and then poof it was gone. I absolutely loved seeing this.

I have seen Jesus three times and feel so unbelievably lucky to have. He appeared at the foot of my bed when I was around 12 years old. He then again appeared to me in the hospital when I had my scare with cancer surgery at age 53. Then months later he appeared in a dream and held a cross up to me. His eyes were magnificent.

Being clairvoyant has warned me and others of pending danger. I was working and saw a quick picture flash of a car accident. It was very quick and I was busy and not driving so I kept on working. Then the next day I was driving home from Manhattan and I heard a voice say, "Be careful move over." I stayed in my lane a little longer and then heard, "Move!" loud and clear. I actually cut the person off next to me and moved over to the other lane. The truck that had been in front of me in the other lane crashed into the car in front of it and all the cars behind were in a chain crash. It would have been me first behind that truck had I not heard the message and moved over. Spirits know I will listen to them so they come in loud and clear when they need to. They know I will also give others their messages. I actually see images that make no sense to me but do for the person the message is for.

Visions will occur anywhere and anytime. I was out to dinner with my boyfriend and got up to use the rest room. In the bathroom while washing my hands, there stood an apparition behind me. I turned around and I saw her walk through the door. It was startling to say the least and I went back to the table. I immediately start telling my boyfriend and then the waitress comes over. I interrupt her telling us the specials of the day and tell her I'm psychic and saw an apparition in the bathroom. I stated that I saw what she was wearing and what she looked like. The waitress said she would be right back. The owner comes over with her and asks me to describe what I saw. She had a black dress on with a white bib apron over top. She had funny looking shoe boots on. She was a plump full woman and her hair was up and covered. I said she's still here and talking to me. She's saying that she owned this place and there was a fire and children died here too. The owner was amazed. He said he would be right back. He came back with an old book with photos in it. He asked me to browse through it. As I browse through these old photos I stop on a page where I saw this exact woman's photo. I said, "This is her, this is the apparition that was in the bathroom." It was exact to the shoes. Then the owner asks if I can get her name? I ask spirit what her name was and I kept hearing DDDDDD. I looked up and said all I'm getting is the letter D over and over. He was floored. Her name was Dolores and it was known she was called Dee.

I did go back to that restaurant with friends a few months later. My friend and I were sitting by the wall and had our picture taken. When we saw the picture, a spirit was behind us and clearlyvisible.

This picture has been disturbing to me and I simply don't know what this is, but there is definitely a spirit behind me and over my head, that seems to resemble a child.

It is quite rare and often difficult to discern Spirits in photos. Most people write them off as bad lighting or dust. As another example of Spirit being seen in a photo there is what seems to be a beautiful Angel spirit captured at my friend Virginia's house. She too is a medium and she sent me a picture of an angel she caught on camera.

I am always amazed by seeing something that is a sign from the other side. I believe that we are supposed to share these moments of wonder and keep the door open for those who are skeptics and for those who are just not spiritual. I am not the type of person to want to change anyone's beliefs, just to allow what is and to present it for each individual to take from it whatever it is they take.

Just recently, I smelled my mothers' perfume in my kitchen area. It was very strong and caught me by surprise. I never really liked that perfume either. I turned around and felt her there right next to me and the smell stayed for another 3 seconds and then it was gone. It is so wonderful to live knowing and experiencing all this. Two days later my sister Denise who lives in Arizona called to tell me that she smelled our Mom's perfume by her living room window. My sister didn't like that perfume either. I said I smelled it too on the same day. Our mom absolutely came to visit both of us to let us know that she is still with us.

I have experienced and seen enough now that even if I didn't want to believe in this spiritual world it wouldn't be possible. I believe a strong faith can and will get you through anything. Seeing signs or apparitions or smelling something out of nowhere is a way that Spirit comes to you. Open up your world to this and maybe you too will have beautiful experiences. For those who are psychic and spiritual already, sharing experiences always help others and help spread the wonderment of our existence.

I believe we all have many Angels that watch over us and nudge us along the way. If you want to see or hear from them simply start talking to them and ask. Clear you mind and thoughts through mediation and do not let anything interrupt this quiet space. They will come to you. Only a real and strong belief in them will allow this to actually happen. I feel if you are just looking to see or hear them for affirmation that they exist, it probably won't happen. I have always believed and had an inner embodiment of 'knowing' it all exists. I can't always explain perfectly how or why, I just know.

Being both highly spiritual and psychic makes me even more sensitive to my surroundings. On the psychic side the four main 'clairs' are clairvoyance, clairaudience, claircognizance, and clairsentience.

The 'Clairs' meanings are as follows:

Clairvoyance, "Clear Seeing": Experiencing seeing metaphorical images/visions.

Clairaudience, "Clear Hearing": Experiencing hearing voices or sounds.

Claircognizance, "Clear Knowing": You just know something without any other proofs.

Clairsentience, "Clear Feeling": Experiencing a feeling. Sometimes I can feel how a person has died.

Clairalience, "Clear Smell": Experiencing a smell out of nowhere that is from Spirit letting you know they are still around.

You may experience one, some or all of these. Try to listen to your inner voice which is part of your psychic intelligence. How to do this is simple. Meditate into your 'clairs' and look, listen, know and feel what is around or inside you. Along with this, call upon your Angels and Spirit Guides to also assist, guide and send messages. If you want to see and know more so that you can be a better person or obtain a better life or whatever it is you may be seeking, allow your psychic intelligence to help you obtain it. Along with prayer and speaking to your Angels and Spirit Guides you will see remarkable changes occur. Angels are here to protect us. You may ask why sometimes bad things still happen. Well, the answer is that we are supposed to learn a lesson from that negative experience. Spirit guides again, are those you have already had a previous earthly connection to and have passed on. I recommend you call upon them also. Both Angels and spirit guides need to hear from us. They want to hear from us. Can you imagine that you are given all this help and influence and you don't even use it? Can you imagine how they feel on the other side with you not talking to them or seeking advice and guidance? Also, thank them and acknowledge the service they give you. It is top notch and the absolute best you're going to get.

So, take one day at time and try to stay open and positive to whatever happens in life. Work on opening yourself to your own psychic abilities and rely on your Angels and Spirit Guides. Surround yourself with positivity, make smart and realistic goals, don't compare yourself to others, believe in yourself, believe in what you see and hear from Spirit and allow it all to happen.